I0007829

AI Marketing Mastery

Expert Secrets to Building a 7-Figure Coaching Business

Lisa Lieberman-Wang

"The Coaches' Coach"

Certified AI Expert &
Business Marketing Strategist

CONTACT

To Book Lisa for Corporate Events
call 1-877-250-7275

For more information, go to
www.LisaLiebermanWang.com

For most current book alumnus promotions see

www.LisaLiebermanWang.com

FIRST EDITON

Author: Lisa Lieberman-Wang, "AI Marketing Mastery - Expert Secrets to Building a 7-Figure Coaching Business"

ISBN# 9798333694096

Table of Contents

Here's What Leaders in The Coaching Industry Are Saying

"Using Lisa's signature formula, her 7-figure talk process, and her deep dive into what people really need, want, and desire, she showed me how to help provide that value and that transaction to them. I've been able to generate millions, that's right seven figures in sales. Now she is teaching people how to do it with AI and it is blowing up people's businesses."

– Jerremy Newsome,
Stock Expert, Real Life Trading

"WOW! Lisa Lieberman-Wang is the real deal and a legit AI and marketing superstar. I worked with her on my first mastermind, and together we crushed a six-figure talk that sold incredibly well. With all candor, I'm normally underwhelmed by other people's level of work commitment. But working with Lisa was so different; it was refreshing. At every opportunity, she went above and beyond to make sure all the fine details were executed to completion. Because of Lisa, the results we generated together were phenomenal. Her abilities, strategies, and willingness to optimize are among the many reasons I'm going to be working with Lisa for many years to come."

– Todd Hartley, CEO of WireBuzz,
Tony Robbins Business Mastery Speaker

"I've been working with Lisa for almost a decade, and she's consistently kept me on the cutting edge of marketing trends. AI is no exception. Lisa introduced me to AI tools before they became mainstream, giving me a significant advantage. I've developed skills few others possess, creating custom GPTs and becoming a valuable resource for leveraging AI in marketing. Her strategies have resulted in over 520% ROI on coaching services. Lisa's new book covers everything from creating content at scale to mastering AI for in-depth marketing gains, instrumental in my own business growth. If you're looking to build a seven-figure coaching business with cutting-edge AI strategies, this book is a must-read."

Irena Fisher,
CEO Averista, Marketing Experts

"If you are someone like me who has amazing ideas that they want to bring to the world but yet struggles with putting a marketing plan together and getting it launched, then working with Lisa Lieberman-Wang is an absolute no-brainer.

The speed at which Lisa operates and implements AI into her proven "Mastery to Millions" is awe-inspiring. Her ability to know exactly what you need in the moment, how to structure it, and the steps to launch your program is beyond anyone's wildest dreams. Lisa's genius, dedication, devotion, and professionalism to help make you a 7-figure coach truly come from her heart and is incredibly inspirational."

- Ally Jewel,
Sex & Intimacy, & Erotic Blueprint™ Lead Coach

"What has been fascinating for me is to watch Lisa bring such a high level of expertise from so many disciplines, from personal growth and development and the psychology of success to marketing and pragmatic business strategies and weave it all together seamlessly while honestly delivering some of the best content that I've seen in any of those spaces for a lot of years."

– Deb Battersby, Success Matrix,
CEO, Maverick Coaching

"You go to Lisa when you want your mind blown. She's the expert and with AI she brought it to the next level. She has been our board advisor for over a decade, actively helping us with strategic marketing as we built multiple multi-million-dollar businesses in the health and wellness space. Lisa is a true expert in leveraging AI to save lives and grow businesses. This book is a must-read for anyone serious about using AI to transform their business." – Dr. Roger Sahoury, #1 Bestseller, SprintSet Energizing Weight Loss System "

– DR. Roger Sahoury,
#1 Bestseller, SprintSet Energizing Weight Loss System

"Lisa's innovative use of AI has been a game-changer for our business. Her strategic insights helped us transform abstract ideas into thriving ventures with remarkable results. With her guidance, we developed a robust online presence and crafted a marketing strategy that significantly increased our client base and revenue. Thanks to Lisa, our business has seen extraordinary growth. This book will provide you with the same AI-driven strategies to achieve your success."

– Frankie,
Relationship Coach & Hacienda Serena, PR Airbnb Owner

Forward

*W*elcome to the cutting edge of coaching and entrepreneurship. You're about to embark on a journey that will revolutionize your business through the power of Artificial Intelligence. This isn't just another tech manual – it's your personal guide to harnessing AI to build the seven-figure coaching business you've always dreamed of.

As someone who's walked this path, let me share a personal story that illustrates the transformative power of AI in coaching. Just a few years ago, I was where many of you are now – successful but striving for that next level. I was working 60-hour weeks, constantly creating content, managing client relationships, and trying to scale my business. It felt like pushing a boulder uphill.

Then came my AI awakening. I remember the day I first used ChatGPT to help me outline a client proposal. What usually took me hours was done in minutes, and the quality was even better than my usual work. That was my "aha" moment. I realized that AI wasn't just a tool – it was a game-changing partner that could help me scale my impact without scaling my time investment.

From that day on, I dove deep into the world of AI for coaching. I experimented, I learned, and yes, I made mistakes. But the results were undeniable. Within a year, my revenue had doubled, my client satisfaction scores were at an all-time high, and I had reclaimed hours of my week for family, self-care, and strategic thinking.

This book is the culmination of that journey. It's everything I wish I'd known when I started, packed with practical strategies, real-world case studies, and actionable tools you can implement immediately. **You'll learn how to:**

- **Use AI** to create high-converting marketing content in minutes, not hours
- **Leverage AI-powered analytics** to understand your clients better than ever before
- **Scale your impact with AI-assisted coaching tools**, without losing the personal touch
- **Automate the time-consuming parts of your business**, freeing you to focus on what you do best

But more than that, this book is about mindset. It's about seeing AI not as a threat, but as a powerful ally in your mission to change lives. It's about embracing the future of coaching with open arms and an innovative spirit.

As you read, you'll hear not just from me, but from other coaches who've successfully integrated AI into their practices. These aren't outliers – they're a glimpse of what's possible when you harness the power of AI in your coaching business.

So, whether you're a seasoned coach looking to scale, or an entrepreneur ready to leverage AI for growth, this book is your roadmap to success. Get ready to transform your business, amplify your impact, and step confidently into the AI-powered future of coaching.

Let's begin this exciting journey together!

Love, Lisa

Chapter 1
Setting the Stage for Your AI-Powered Coaching Journey

Welcome to the exciting world of AI-powered coaching!

We're about to embark on a transformative journey that will revolutionize your practice. Before we dive into the game-changing strategies, let's lay the groundwork with a friendly AI orientation.

To begin we'll introduce you to the concept of AI in coaching, demystifying key terms and addressing important ethical considerations. You'll discover how AI has evolved in the coaching industry and learn how to prepare yourself for seamlessly integrating these powerful tools into your practice.

Consider this your launchpad - a comprehensive foundation that will get you up to speed and ready for the AI-powered adventures ahead. By the end of this chapter, you'll have a clear understanding of what AI can do for your coaching business and how to approach this technology with confidence and ethical awareness.

So, buckle up and get ready to explore the fascinating intersection of artificial intelligence and coaching. Your journey to becoming an AI-savvy coach starts right here, right now!

The ABCs of AI: A Quick Terminology Guide

Remember when "AI" was just something from science fiction movies? Well, times have changed. Let's break down some key terms you'll encounter in this book:

Artificial Intelligence (AI): Think of AI as a really smart digital assistant. Its software is designed to mimic human intelligence, learning from data to perform tasks that typically require human thinking.

Machine Learning: This is how AI gets smarter. It's like AI's study sessions, where it learns from patterns in data without being explicitly programmed.

Natural Language Processing (NLP): This is AI's ability to understand and generate human language. It's what allows you to have a conversation with ChatGPT or Siri.

Generative AI: This is the creative genius of the AI world. It can create new content, from text to images to video, based on what it's learned.

The Evolution of AI in Coaching: From Sci-Fi to Your Office

Let me take you on a quick trip down memory lane. When I first started coaching, our most advanced tech was probably a fancy Excel spreadsheet. Fast forward to today, and AI is transforming every aspect of our industry.

It started with simple scheduling tools and has evolved into AI that can help create personalized coaching plans, generate content, and even assist in analyzing client progress. I remember the first time I used an AI writing assistant, Quillbot, to help draft a client email. It felt like magic – suddenly, writer's block was a thing of the past!

Ethical Considerations: Keeping it Human in a Digital World

Now, I know what you might be thinking: "Lisa, is AI going to replace coaches?" Let me put your mind at ease – absolutely not! AI is a tool, not a replacement for human empathy and expertise.

However, we do need to use AI responsibly. Always be transparent with your clients about how you're using AI in your practice. Protect their data fiercely, and never rely on AI for critical decisions about a client's well-being. Remember, you're the coach – AI is just your very clever assistant.

AI Limitations: Superman Has Kryptonite, AI Has Its Limits

As amazing as AI is, it's not omniscient. It can make mistakes, exhibit biases, and sometimes generate nonsensical or inappropriate content. I once asked an AI to write a motivational speech, and it came back with a bizarre mix of Shakespeare quotes and cooking tips. Needless to say, I didn't use that in my seminar!

Always review and refine AI-generated content. Use your human judgment – that's something AI can't replace.

Ethical Considerations in AI-Powered Coaching

As we embrace AI in our coaching practices, it's crucial to consider the ethical implications. Here are key ethical considerations to keep in mind:

Transparency: Always be upfront with your clients about your use of AI tools. Explain how AI enhances your coaching but doesn't replace your expertise.

Data Privacy: Ensure that any AI tools you use comply with data protection regulations like GDPR. Be cautious about inputting client information into AI systems.

Bias Awareness: AI can perpetuate biases present in its training data. Be vigilant in reviewing AI-generated content for potential biases.

Maintaining the Human Touch: While AI can enhance efficiency, remember that coaching is fundamentally about human connection. Use AI to supplement, not substitute, your personal interaction with clients.

Continuous Learning: Stay informed about AI developments and their ethical implications in coaching. Regularly reassess your AI use to ensure it aligns with coaching best practices.

Accountability: Remember that you are ultimately responsible for the advice and content you provide, even if AI assisted in its creation.

Informed Consent: Consider obtaining explicit consent from clients regarding your use of AI in your coaching process.

Emotional Intelligence: AI lacks emotional intelligence. Always apply your human judgment, especially in sensitive situations.

Action Step: Create an "AI Ethics Statement" for your coaching practice. Outline how you pledge to use AI responsibly and ethically in your work with clients.

Your AI Readiness Checklist

Before we dive into the nitty-gritty of AI implementation, let's make sure you're ready for this journey:

1. Do you have clear goals for your coaching business?
2. Are you open to experimenting and learning from both successes and failures?
3. Do you have basic tech setup (computer, stable internet, smartphone)?
4. Are you committed to maintaining the human touch in your coaching?
5. Are you ready to invest time in learning new tools?

If you answered yes to these, you're ready to embark on this AI adventure!

How to Read This Book: Your Roadmap to AI Mastery

This isn't a textbook to be read passively. Think of it as a workshop in book form. As you read, try out the tools and techniques. Play with the prompts. Experiment with the strategies. The magic happens when you apply what you learn. You won't break the internet so be willing to go out and have fun testing it all out, you'll be amazed.

Each chapter ends with action steps. Do them! They're your opportunity to implement and see real results in your coaching practice. Imagine I am there with you and you can't progress to the next section until you complete the task. Seriously, you'll be happy you did.

AI Safety and Best Practices: Navigating the Digital Landscape

As we venture into the AI world, let's keep these best practices in mind:

1. Always verify AI-generated information before using it with clients.
2. Regularly update your AI tools to ensure you're using the latest, most secure versions.
3. Keep your clients' data safe – use reputable, secure AI platforms.
4. Maintain a healthy balance between AI assistance and your own expertise.
5. Stay informed about AI developments in the coaching industry.

Embracing a Future-Proof Mindset

The AI landscape is evolving rapidly. What's cutting-edge today might be outdated tomorrow. But don't let that intimidate you. Instead, cultivate a mindset of continuous learning and adaptability.

I remember feeling overwhelmed when I first started incorporating AI into my practice. But I approached it with curiosity rather than fear. Each new tool was an opportunity to enhance my coaching, not a threat to my expertise.

As we embark on this journey together, keep an open mind. Be ready to adapt, to learn, and to grow. The future of coaching is AI-enhanced, and by reading this book, you're positioning yourself at the forefront of this exciting revolution.

Are you ready to transform your coaching practice with AI? Let's dive in!

Key Takeaways:

- Understanding AI basics is crucial for implementing it effectively in coaching
- AI is a tool to enhance, not replace, human coaching skills
- Adopting a growth mindset is essential for success with AI in coaching

Introduction: Transforming Your Coaching Business with AI

*P*icture this: It's Monday morning, and you wake up to find that while you were sleeping, your AI assistant has drafted three personalized client session plans, created a week's worth of social media content, and analyzed your latest campaign data to suggest improvements. This isn't science fiction – it's the reality of running an AI-powered coaching business in 2024.

Welcome to the future of coaching. If you're reading this, you're already successful. You've built a prosperous business through hard work, dedication, and a genuine passion for helping others. But something inside you knows there's another level – a seven-figure level – and you're ready to reach it.

Here's the thing: the path from six to seven figures isn't just about working harder. It's about working smarter, and that's where AI comes in.

Let me share a quick story of transformation:

"I was initially skeptical about AI, but Lisa's guidance completely changed my perspective. As my coach for years, Lisa has always been ahead of the curve with invaluable tips and new trends, and AI was no exception. Introducing AI into my business has been transformative, saving me time and energy while maintaining my authentic voice. Tasks that once took weeks or days now only take hours or minutes. As an author and writer for several publications, AI has made it even easier to get my message out. Thanks to AI, I can create more tailored content for my ideal clients and provide a noticeably higher level of service. I can't imagine running my coaching business without it now!"

– Lois Kramer-Perez,
Feng Shui Expert

This book is your roadmap to achieving similar (and even better) results. In the following chapters, we'll delve into giving you the necessary tools and resources.

When I first started integrating AI into my coaching business, I was excited. I thought, "How can a machine help me deliver the personal touch my clients expect?" So I decided to experiment. I used AI to help me create a personalized welcome sequence for new clients. The result? My client retention rate shot up, and referrals increased. Why? Because the AI helped me deliver more personalized, timely content than I ever could manually, freeing me up to focus on high-impact Strategy sessions with my clients.

This book is your roadmap to achieving similar (and even better) results.

In the coming segments, we will delve further into:

1. **Mindset Mastery:** How to adopt an AI-positive growth mindset that sets you up for success.
2. **Client Avatar Precision:** Using AI to identify and target your ideal high-ticket clients with laser focus.
3. **High-Ticket Program Design:** Leveraging AI to create irresistible premium offerings that sell themselves.
4. **AI-Powered Branding:** Building a magnetic brand identity that stands out in a crowded market.
5. **Marketing Magic:** Harnessing AI for personalized, high-impact marketing campaigns that fill your pipeline.
6. **Sales Funnel Optimization:** Designing AI-driven funnels that convert leads into high-ticket clients on autopilot.
7. **Seamless Communication:** Using AI to automate and enhance client engagement with a personal touch.
8. **Content Creation at Scale:** Producing endless streams of engaging content without burning out.
9. **Video Marketing Mastery:** Leveraging AI to create compelling video content that builds trust and authority.
10. **The AI-Assisted Book:** Using AI to write and market your own book, establishing yourself as the go-to expert in your niche.

Each chapter is packed with actionable strategies, real-world case studies, and step-by-step guides to implementing AI in your coaching business. You'll hear from coaches who used AI-powered analytics to identify underserved niches and others who leveraged AI content creation tools to draft scripts for videos they did on Tik Toc and Instagram and got hundreds of thousands of views.

But this book isn't just about theory. At the end of each chapter, you'll find an "Action Steps" section with specific tools to try and exercises to complete. By the time you n this book, you won't just have knowledge – you'll have a fully implemented AI strategy working for your business 24/7.

A word of caution: this book isn't magic. It won't transform your business overnight. What it will do is give you the tools, strategies, and mindset to leverage AI in a way that amplifies your unique gifts as a coach.

Remember, AI is here to enhance your coaching, not replace it. Your empathy, intuition, and human connection are still your greatest assets – AI just helps you deliver them on a scale.

So, are you ready to step into the future of coaching? To work smarter, not harder? To impact more lives while enjoying more freedom on your own? Then let's dive in. Your seven-figure AI-powered coaching business awaits!

Getting Started with AI

Understanding AI and Prompts: The Basics

Before we dive into the transformative power of AI in coaching, let's break down what AI is and how you can effectively communicate with it.

What is AI?

Expanding on what I started sharing earlier, Artificial Intelligence, or AI, is like a super-smart digital assistant. It's computer software designed to mimic human intelligence, learning from data and experiences to perform tasks that typically require human cognition. In the context of this book, we're primarily talking about language models like ChatGPT or Claude, which can understand and generate human-like text.

What is a Prompt?

A prompt is simply the input you give to an AI. **It's like asking a question** or **giving instructions** to a very capable assistant. The quality and specificity of your prompt largely determine the usefulness of the AI's output.

How Prompts Work?

When you enter a prompt, the AI analyzes it, draws upon its vast knowledge base, and generates a response. The clearer and more specific your prompt, the better the AI can understand your needs and provide relevant output.

Crafting Effective Prompts: The CREATE Method

To get the best results from AI, use the CREATE method when writing your prompts:

   C - Context: Provide background information and set the scene.

   R - Result: Clearly state what you want to achieve or create.

   E - Explanation: Ask for details or reasoning behind the AI's output.

A - Audience: Specify who the content is for.

T - Tone: Indicate the desired style or voice.

E - Expand: Ask the AI to elaborate on specific points or ideas.

Example:

Poor prompt: "Give me marketing ideas."

Better prompt (using CREATE):

Context: I'm a life coach launching a new online program for working mothers.

Result: I need 5 innovative marketing strategies to promote this program.

Explanation: For each strategy, provide a brief rationale on why it would be effective. Audience: The content should appeal to busy working mothers aged 35-40.

Tone: Use an empathetic and motivational voice.

Expand: Include at least one social media strategy and one email marketing tactic."

This improved prompt provides Context about the business and program, clearly states the desired Result of 5 marketing strategies, asks for an Explanation of each strategy's effectiveness, specifies the Audience as working mothers, sets a Tone that's empathetic and motivational, and asks to Expand on specific types of marketing tactics.

By understanding these basics and applying the CREATE method, you'll be well-equipped to harness the power of AI in your coaching business. Throughout this book, we'll provide numerous examples of effective prompts for various aspects of your coaching practice.

Power Prompts

Remember those **Mad Libs games** we played as kids? Well, we're about to play a grown-up version that's going to supercharge your coaching business. But instead of silly stories, we're creating powerful prompts that will transform your business.

Think of these prompts as your personal Mad Libs for success, powered by our trusty **CREATE method**.

Now, in each prompt, you'll see brackets like [your niche] or [your current revenue] - that's where you fill in your specific information. This personalization, combined with the CREATE method, is what makes these prompts so powerful. It's like having a custom-tailored AI assistant that knows your business inside and out and speaks your language.

Here's a quick example of how this works:

Context: [I'm a life coach specializing in career transitions]

Result: Create a content plan for the next month

Explanation: Include the rationale behind each content piece

Audience: [My ideal clients are professionals in their 30s looking to switch careers]

Tone: Motivational and practical

Expand: Provide ideas for repurposing each piece of content across different platforms

See how filling in those brackets personalizes the prompt? And how does following the CREATE method ensure you get comprehensive, tailored results?

So, grab your metaphorical pencil (or just your keyboard), and let's start filling in those blanks and "CREATEing" your success. With each prompt you complete, you're one step closer to that seven-figure coaching business you've been dreaming of.

Ready to play? Let's dive in and start creating your success story, one AI-powered prompt at a time!

Key Takeaways:

- Understanding AI basics is crucial for implementing it effectively in coaching
- AI is a tool to enhance, not replace, human coaching skills
- Adopting a growth mindset is essential for success with AI in coaching
- AI can revolutionize every aspect of your coaching practice
- The path from six to seven figures involves working smarter with AI
- AI helps deliver more personalized, timely content and services

Action Steps:

1. **Conduct a personal AI readiness assessment.** Review the AI Readiness Checklist provided here and honestly evaluate where you stand on each point.
2. **Choose one AI tool** mentioned in the chapter (e.g., ChatGPT, Claude, or Jasper) and sign up for a free trial or start using it.
3. **Identify one repetitive task** in your coaching business that takes up a lot of your time. Research how AI could potentially help automate or streamline this task.

4. **Create an "AI Learning Journal"** where you can document your experiences, insights, and questions as you start incorporating AI into your coaching practice.

5. **Join an online community or forum** where coaches discuss their experiences with AI. This could be a LinkedIn group, Facebook group, or a dedicated AI for coaches. We have one here on WhatsApp. Scan the QR Code to Join Us Now!

Chapter 2
Unleashing The Power of AI in Coaching

You have now entered the cutting edge of coaching innovation. We're going to explore how Artificial Intelligence is revolutionizing the coaching industry, and more importantly, how you can harness its power to transform your business. As someone who's been in the trenches of personal development and business strategy for decades, I can tell you with certainty: AI is not just another passing trend. It's the future, and that future is now.

The AI Revolution in Coaching

Let's start by addressing the elephant in the room. When most people hear "AI," they might think of sci-fi movies or fear that robots are coming to take their jobs. But here's the truth: AI is not here to replace coaches. It's here to empower us, to amplify our capabilities, and to help us reach more people with our message.

Think about it this way. In the past, if you wanted to create content, design a marketing strategy, or even write a book, you had two options: do it yourself (which could take months or even years) or hire a team of experts (which could cost tens of thousands of dollars). Now, with AI, you have a third option: a powerful tool that can help you accomplish these tasks in a fraction of the time and cost.

But it's not just about efficiency. AI is also about effectiveness. It can help you understand your audience better, craft more compelling messages, and deliver your coaching in ways that resonate more deeply with your clients. In essence, AI is like having a team of expert assistants at your fingertips, ready to help you with everything from content creation to market research.

The Transformative Potential of AI

Let me share a personal story to illustrate the transformative power of AI. When I first started my coaching business, I was like many of you -- passionate about helping people but struggling with the business side of things. I spent countless hours trying to figure out my niche, create content, and market my services. I paid experts thousands of dollars to do what I felt they did better than me. It was like pushing a boulder uphill.

Fast forward to today. With the help of AI, I can accomplish in hours what used to take weeks. For example, when I was writing my latest book on building a seven-figure coaching business, I used AI to help me outline the chapters, generate ideas, and even draft sections of the content. What would have taken months of work was completed in a matter of weeks.

But here's the key: AI didn't write the book for me. It was a tool that helped me express my ideas more effectively and efficiently. The insights, the strategies, the personal stories -- those all came from me. AI simply helped me put it all together in a compelling way.

Why AI is the Game-Changer for Your Coaching Business

Let's break it down:

1. **Personalization at Scale:** AI allows you to personalize your coaching services for each client, even as you scale your business. It can help you analyze client data, identify patterns, and suggest personalized strategies for everyone.

2. **Content Creation:** Writer's block? Thing of the past. AI can help you generate ideas for blog posts, social media content, and even entire books. It's like having a brainstorming partner available 24/7.

3. **Market Research:** Understanding your target audience is crucial for any business. AI can analyze vast amounts of data to give you insights into your ideal client's needs, wants, and behaviors.

4. **Automated Administrative Tasks:** Let's face it, as coaches, we'd rather spend our time coaching. AI can handle many of the administrative tasks that eat up our time, from scheduling appointments to sending follow-up emails.

5. **Enhanced Decision Making:** AI can process and analyze data much faster than humans, providing you with insights to make better business decisions.

6. **Improved Client Experience:** From chatbots that can answer client queries 24/7 to AI-driven tools that can track client progress, AI can significantly enhance the client experience.

7. **Continuous Learning:** AI doesn't sleep. It's constantly learning and improving, which means your AI tools will get better over time, providing you with ever-improving insights and assistance.

Real-World Success Stories

1. **AI-Powered Virtual Assistants in Customer Service:** Instacart Storefront utilizes AI-driven cognitive virtual assistants to provide consistent, personalized, and instant responses to customer inquiries. When more complex issues arise, the system seamlessly transitions to human customer service representatives. This integration ensures a high level of personalized customer service around the clock, improving client satisfaction and engagement.

   Coaches can adopt similar AI-powered virtual assistants to handle routine client interactions, freeing up more time for personalized coaching sessions.

2. **AI-Enhanced Personalization and Client Insights:** Hilton employs IBM Watson for an AI-powered concierge service that offers individualized recommendations to guests. By analyzing guest preferences, Watson helps Hilton fine-tune room amenities and services, creating a tailored experience for each visitor.

   Similarly, coaches can leverage AI-supported analytics to gain deeper insights into their clients' preferences and behaviors, enabling them to offer more personalized and effective coaching services.

3. **AI in Real-Time Client Engagement:** Georgia State University introduced an AI chatbot named Pounce to help reduce "summer melt" (students enrolled in spring dropping out by fall). Pounce uses conversational AI technology to provide real-time, personalized responses to student queries, helping them navigate enrollment processes and stay engaged. This initiative led to a 22% reduction in summer melt.

   Coaches can implement similar AI-driven engagement tools to maintain constant, supportive communication with clients, ensuring they stay motivated and on track with their goals. Know the future is here and now.

Overcoming the AI Learning Curve

Now, I know what some of you might be thinking. "Lisa, this all sounds great, but I'm not a tech expert. How am I supposed to use AI?"

First, let me assure you: you don't need to be a tech wizard to benefit from AI. Many AI tools are designed to be user-friendly, with intuitive interfaces that anyone can learn to use.

Second, remember this: the time you invest in learning to use AI tools will pay off exponentially. It's like learning to drive a car. It might seem daunting at first, but once you've mastered it, it opens up a world of possibilities.

Here are some steps you can take to start incorporating AI into your coaching business:

1. **Start Small:** Don't try to overhaul your entire business overnight. Start with one area, like content creation or market research, and gradually expand from there.

2. **Experiment:** Many AI tools offer free trials. Take advantage of these to experiment and find the tools that work best for you.

3. **Stay Curious:** The field of AI is constantly evolving. Stay curious and keep learning about new developments and applications in the coaching industry.

4. **Focus on Your Strengths:** Remember, AI is here to enhance your skills, not replace them. Focus on using AI to amplify your unique strengths as a coach.

5. **Ethical Considerations:** As we embrace AI, it's crucial to consider the ethical implications. Always be transparent with your clients about how you're using AI in your coaching practice.

The Future of Coaching with AI

As we look to the future, the possibilities are truly exciting. Imagine AI-powered virtual reality coaching sessions, where you can create immersive experiences for your clients. Or AI tools that can predict potential challenges your clients might face and suggest preemptive strategies.

But here's the most important thing to remember at its core, coaching is about human connection. AI will never replace the empathy, intuition, and personal touch that you bring to your coaching. What it will do is free you up to focus more on these uniquely human aspects of coaching, while handling many of the time-consuming tasks that currently eat up your day.

In the coming chapters, we'll dive deep into specific strategies and tools you can use to leverage AI in every aspect of your coaching business. From creating your perfect client avatar to designing high-ticket programs, from crafting compelling content to building high-converting funnels -- we'll cover it all.

But for now, I want you to do one thing: open your mind to the possibilities. The AI revolution in coaching is here, and it's up to you to decide whether you'll be at the forefront or playing catch-up.

Remember, success leaves clues. The most successful coaches and entrepreneurs are already leveraging AI to grow their businesses and impact more lives. It's time for you to join them.

Following we'll explore how to cultivate the right mindset for success in this new AI-powered coaching landscape. Because while AI is a powerful tool, it's your mindset that will ultimately determine your success.

Are you ready to unleash the power of AI in your coaching business? Let's go!

Key Takeaways:

- AI can amplify your coaching capabilities and reach
- Key areas for AI application include content creation, market research, and client communication
- Overcoming the AI learning curve is essential for success

Action Steps:

1. **Reflect on your current business processes.** Which areas take up most of your time? These might be prime candidates for AI assistance.
2. **Set a goal** to implement at least one AI tool in your business within the next month. Start small but start now.

Remember, the journey of a thousand miles begins with a single step. Your journey to AI mastery in your coaching business starts now. Let's make it count!

Chapter 3
Crafting Your AI Dream Team: Mastering Custom GPT Prompts

$\mathcal{S}$ee it now: It's Monday morning, and you're gearing up to create a new marketing strategy for your coaching business. You open ChatGPT, and... you're staring at a blank prompt. Again. You spend the next hour trying to remember all the specific instructions and context you need to provide to get a useful response. Sound familiar?

Now, imagine instead that you have a **custom AI assistant** that already knows your business, your style, and your goals. You simply ask, "What's the best marketing strategy for my new group coaching program?" and boom! You get a tailored response that feels like it came from a dream team of marketing experts.

This, my friend, is the power of **Custom GPT prompts**. We are now going to help you learn how you can create your very own AI dream team.

Why Custom GPTs Matter

When I first started using AI in my business, I found myself repeating the same context over and over again. It was like having a new intern every single day who knew nothing about my business. Frustrating, right?

That's when I discovered the magic of Custom GPTs. By creating personalized AI assistants, I was able to save countless hours and dramatically improve the quality of AI-generated content. It was like finally having a seasoned team member who understood my business inside and out.

Creating Your AI Board of Advisors

One of the most powerful applications of Custom GPTs is creating your own dream team of experts who are available 24/7 to advise you on various aspects of your business.

Here's an example of how I created my marketing advisory board:

Marketing Advisors

1. Lisa Lieberman-Wang

- **Expertise:** Sales, Marketing, Emotional Intelligence
- **Platform:** Mastery to Millions, 7 Figure Talks That Sell, How to Build a 7 Figure Coaching Business
- **Role:** Advisor on integrating emotional intelligence, understanding human psychology with extensive experience and success with strategic marketing and sales.

2. Russell Brunson

- **Expertise:** Sales Funnels, Digital Marketing
- **Platform:** ClickFunnels
- **Role:** Advisor on creating effective sales funnels and optimizing the customer journey.

3. Donald Miller

- **Expertise:** Branding, Marketing Strategy
- **Platform:** StoryBrand
- **Role:** Advisor on brand messaging and storytelling frameworks.

4. Todd Hartley

- **Expertise:** Video Marketing
- **Platform:** WireBuzz
- **Role:** Advisor on leveraging video content for marketing and engagement.

5. Tony Robbins

- **Expertise:** Personal Development, Business Strategy
- **Platform:** Tony Robbins' Programs
- **Role:** Advisor on mindset, personal development, and actionable business strategies.

6. Dean Graziosi

- **Expertise:** Real Estate, Personal Development, Marketing
- **Platform:** Mastermind.com
- **Role:** Advisor on leveraging personal stories and building communities.

7. Gary Vaynerchuk

- **Expertise:** Social Media Marketing, Digital Marketing
- **Platform:** VaynerMedia
- **Role:** Advisor on social media strategy and authentic engagement.

8. Neil Patel

- **Expertise:** SEO, Digital Marketing
- **Platform:** Neil Patel Digital
- **Role:** Advisor on increasing online visibility and driving traffic.

9. Jeff Walker

- **Expertise:** Product Launches
- **Platform:** Product Launch Formula
- **Role:** Advisor on product launch strategies and building anticipation.

10. NasDaily (Nuseir Yassin)

- **Expertise:** Social Media Content, Storytelling
- **Platform:** NasDaily
- **Role:** Advisor on creating viral content and engaging storytelling for social media.

11. Brendan Kane

- **Expertise:** Social Media Growth, Digital Strategies
- **Platform:** One Million Followers
- **Role:** Advisor on rapid social media growth and innovative digital marketing strategies.

By creating this board of advisors, I essentially crafted a Custom GPT that could draw upon the collective wisdom of these marketing giants. When I need advice on creating effective sales funnels, I can channel Russell Brunson's expertise. When I'm working on my brand messaging, I can tap into Donald Miller's storytelling frameworks.

Making Your Custom GPT Your Digital Twin

Creating a Custom GPT that truly understands you and your business is like creating a digital twin. The more information you feed it, the more accurate and valuable its outputs will be. Remember the old computer programming adage: GIGO - Garbage In, Garbage Out. If you want exceptional results, you need to input exceptional information.

Collect everything you have and enter it into your own customized GPT. Be generous, given the more you provide the more accurate and personalized your responses will be, as opposed to generic responses that everyone else will receive if they do not do this work first.

Here's how to make your Custom GPT as smart and 'you' as possible:

Business Fundamentals

Mission and Vision Statements: Load these in verbatim. They encapsulate your core purpose and future aspirations.

Company History: Include key milestones, pivotal moments, and the story of how you started your coaching business.

Core Values: These guide your decision-making and should influence your GPT's responses.

Ideal Client Avatar

Detailed Description: Include demographics, psychographics, behaviors, and pain points.

Client Journey Map: How clients typically progress through your services.

Frequently Asked Questions: This helps the GPT understand common concerns and how you address them.

Your Unique Voice and Style

Blog Posts: Especially those that tell your story or showcase your unique perspective.

Social Media Content: Particularly posts that have resonated well with your audience.

Transcripts of Speeches or Presentations: These capture your spoken style and thought processes.

Your Expertise and Methodologies

Books or E-books You've Written: These are gold mines of your structured thoughts and expertise.

Course Materials: Syllabi, lesson plans, and key concepts from your coaching programs.

Proprietary Frameworks or Models: Detailed explanations of any unique approaches you use in your coaching. (Note: When on "open AI" your content can become public access. If you already have content out there on social and the internet realize it is already public. There are closed AI platforms for a fee.)

Multimedia Content

Video Transcripts: From your YouTube channel, reels, or webinars. These often contain off-the-cuff insights that aren't in your written materials.

Podcast Transcripts: If you host or have been a guest on podcasts, include these for additional context and style.

Slide Decks: PowerPoint or other presentation materials, which often contain concise, key points.

Client Interactions

Case Studies: Detailed accounts of how you've helped clients (with identifying information removed).

Testimonials: These highlight the results and experiences clients value most.

Common Objections and Your Responses: How you typically handle doubts or concerns.

Industry Knowledge

Relevant Articles or Research Papers: Especially if you've contributed to or frequently reference them.

Conference Presentations: Both the ones you've given and ones you find particularly influential.

Competitor Analysis: Information about how you differentiate yourself in the market.

Business Processes

Service Descriptions: Detailed breakdowns of what you offer and how you deliver it.

Pricing Strategies: How you structure your offers and determine value.

Marketing Funnels: The journey you take prospects on before they become clients.

Future Plans and Goals

Strategic Plans: Where you see your business going in the next 1-5 years.

Upcoming Launches or New Offers: Information about services or products you're developing.

Personal Touch

Your Biography: A comprehensive version that includes personal anecdotes and professional journey.

Personal Philosophy: Your outlook on life, business, and coaching.

Favorite Quotes or Books: These often influence your thinking and advice.

When uploading all this information, organize it clearly and provide context. You might say something like, "The following is a transcript from my keynote speech at [Conference Name]. It exemplifies my speaking style and core message on [Topic]."

Remember, creating a truly comprehensive Custom GPT is not a one-time task. As your business evolves, as you gain new insights, or as you create new content, continually update your GPT. Think of it as an ever-growing, ever-learning digital version of yourself.

Step-by-Step Guide to Creating Custom GPTs

Now that you know what to include, let's walk through the process of creating your Custom GPT:

1. **Choose Your GPT's Purpose:** Be specific about what you want your AI assistant to help with. Is it for content creation? Marketing strategy? Client communication?

2. **Gather Your Materials:** Collect all the relevant information as outlined in the previous section.

3. **Organize Your Information:** Create a clear structure for your data. This might be chronological, by topic, or by importance.

4. **Write Clear Instructions:** Provide explicit guidelines for how you want the GPT to use this information. For example, "When discussing marketing strategies, prioritize ideas that align with our company values of authenticity and innovation."

5. **Provide Examples:** Give sample prompts and responses to guide the AI's output. This helps calibrate its tone and style.

6. **Test and Refine:** Once your Custom GPT is set up, test it with various prompts. Analyze the responses and refine your instructions or input data as needed.

Best Practices for Custom GPT Prompts

Be Clear and Specific: The more precise your instructions, the better the output.

Use Consistent Language: Try to maintain consistency in terminology and phrasing throughout your inputs.

Regular Updates: Set a schedule to review and update your Custom GPT with new information or insights.

Ethical Considerations: Ensure your Custom GPT adheres to ethical guidelines and respects intellectual property.

Balance Personality and Professionalism: While you want your GPT to sound like you, ensure it maintains a professional tone appropriate for business communication.

Real-World Applications for Custom GPT's for Coaches

1. **Content Creation Assistant:** Create a Custom GPT that understands your voice and can help generate blog posts, social media content, and email newsletters.
2. **Client Onboarding Specialist:** Develop an AI assistant that knows your coaching process inside out and can help streamline client onboarding.
3. **Marketing Strategy Advisor:** Like my marketing advisory board, create a Custom GPT that can provide tailored marketing advice based on expert knowledge.
4. **Program Development Aid:** Use a Custom GPT to help brainstorm new coaching programs or refine existing ones based on your methodologies and client needs.
5. **Personal Brand Consultant:** Create a GPT that understands your personal brand and can help maintain consistency across all your communications.

Measuring and Optimizing Your Custom GPTs

To ensure your Custom GPTs are truly adding value:

1. **Track Time Savings:** Monitor how much time you're saving on tasks that your GPT now handles.
2. **Quality Assessment:** Regularly review the outputs for accuracy and alignment with your brand voice.
3. **Client Feedback:** If you're using GPT-generated content in client interactions, gather feedback on its effectiveness.

4. **Comparative Analysis:** Compare the performance of GPT-assisted tasks with your previous methods.

Use these insights to continually refine and improve your AI assistants.

Future-Proofing Your AI Team

As AI technology evolves, so should your Custom GPTs. Stay updated with the latest advancements in AI and regularly audit your AI team to ensure they're providing the best possible assistance. Consider joining our AI-focused communities to stay abreast of new developments and best practices.

Key Takeaways:

- **Custom GPTs** are like creating a digital version of yourself and your business, saving you time and improving AI outputs.

- **Building an AI "board of advisors"** lets you tap into expert knowledge on demand, enhancing your decision-making and strategies.

- The **more information you feed** your Custom GPT, the smarter and more 'you' it becomes – remember, quality in means quality out.

- **Creating a Custom GPT is an ongoing process** – regularly update it with new information to keep it current and effective.

- **Custom GPTs can be applied** to various aspects of your coaching business, from content creation to marketing strategy and client onboarding.

Action Steps:

1. **Identify three areas** in your coaching business where a Custom GPT could be beneficial.

2. **Create your own board of advisors** for one of these areas, following the example provided.

3. Gather and organize all the relevant information about your business as outlined in the **"Making Your Custom GPT Your Digital Twin"** section.

4. **Develop a Custom GPT** based on this information and test it out on a specific task.

5. **Review the results** and refine your Custom GPT as needed.

6. **Set a regular schedule** (monthly or quarterly) to update and optimize your Custom GPT.

Remember, creating Custom GPTs is an iterative process. Don't be afraid to experiment, learn, and refine. With time and effort, you'll have an AI dream team that propels your coaching business to new heights of efficiency and success.

Now, go forth and create your AI dream team! Your future self – the one with a thriving, AI-enhanced coaching business – will thank you.

Chapter 4
AI Mindset Mastery: Growth & Modeling Success

As a high-achieving coach and entrepreneur, you already know that success starts in the mind. But in this new era of AI-facilitated coaching, cultivating the right mindset is more crucial than ever. It's not just about embracing technology; it's about adopting a growth mindset that allows you to see possibilities where others see obstacles.

The Growth Mindset in the AI Era

Carol Dweck's concept of the growth mindset has revolutionized how we think about learning and achievement. In the context of AI and coaching, this mindset is your secret weapon. It's the belief that your abilities can be developed through dedication and hard work—that your intelligence and talents are just the starting point.

In the rapidly evolving landscape of AI, a growth mindset is non-negotiable. The tools and technologies available to us are changing at breakneck speed. What worked yesterday might be obsolete tomorrow. But with a growth mindset, you'll see these changes not as threats, but as opportunities to learn, grow, and innovate.

Consider this: When ChatGPT was released, some coaches saw it as a threat to their business. But those with a growth mindset saw it differently. They asked, "How can I use this tool to enhance my coaching? How can it help me serve my clients better?" These are the coaches who are now leading the pack, using AI to create more value for their clients and scale their businesses in ways they never thought possible.

Modeling Success: Learning from AI-Savvy Coaches

One of the most powerful ways to develop a growth mindset is to model those who have already achieved what you aspire to. In the world of AI-powered coaching, some pioneers are blazing the trail. While we can't name specific individuals, let's look at some archetypes of successful AI-savvy coaches:

1. **The Efficiency Expert:** This coach has mastered the art of using AI to streamline their business operations. They've automated everything from appointment scheduling to follow-up emails, freeing up their time to focus on high-value activities like one-on-one coaching and program development.

2. **The Content Creator:** This coach leverages AI to produce a constant stream of high-quality, engaging content. They use AI tools for idea generation, content outlining, and even first drafts, allowing them to maintain a strong online presence without burning out.

3. **The Data-Driven Coach:** This coach uses AI-powered analytics to gain deep insights into their clients' needs and behaviors. They use this data to personalize their coaching programs, resulting in better outcomes for their clients and higher retention rates.

4. **The Innovation Pioneer:** This coach is always on the cutting edge, experimenting with new AI tools and technologies. They're not afraid to try new things, and their willingness to innovate has led to breakthrough coaching methodologies that set them apart in their niche.

5. **The Scalability Master:** This coach has used AI to scale their business beyond the traditional one-on-one coaching model. They've created AI-enhanced online courses, group coaching programs, and digital products that allow them to impact more lives while increasing their revenue.

These archetypes demonstrate different ways coaches are leveraging AI to enhance their businesses. The key is that they all approached AI with curiosity and a willingness to learn, embodying the growth mindset we're discussing.

Techniques for Fostering a Success-Oriented Mindset

Developing a growth mindset isn't just about positive thinking. It requires consistent effort and practical strategies. Here are some techniques you can use to foster a success-oriented mindset in the AI era:

1. **Embrace Challenges:** When you encounter a new AI tool or technology, don't shy away from it. See it as an opportunity to learn and grow. Set yourself the challenge of mastering one new AI tool each month.

2. **Learn from Failure:** If an AI-driven strategy doesn't work out as planned, don't see it as a failure. Instead, ask yourself, "What can I learn from this? How can I improve next time?"

3. **Effort Leads to Mastery:** Remember that mastering AI tools takes time and effort. Celebrate the effort you put in, not just the results you achieve.

4. **Seek Feedback:** Don't be afraid to ask for feedback on your AI strategies. Whether it's from clients, peers, or mentors, constructive feedback is a goldmine for growth.

5. **Find Inspiration in Others' Success:** When you see other coaches succeeding with AI, don't feel threatened. Instead, get inspired and ask yourself, "What can I learn from their approach?"

6. **Continuous Learning:** Make continuous learning a part of your routine. Set aside time each week to read about new AI developments in coaching. Websites like AI Trends or the AI section of Harvard Business Review are great resources.

7. **Reframe Challenges:** Instead of saying "I can't do this," say "I can learn to do this." This simple change in language can shift your entire perspective.

Daily Practices for Mindset Mastery

Cultivating a growth mindset requires daily practice. Here are some exercises you can incorporate into your daily routine:

1. **Morning Mindset Ritual:** Start your day by writing down three ways you can use AI to grow your coaching business today.

2. **Gratitude for Growth:** Each evening, reflect on one thing you learned about AI or how it helped your business that day.

3. **Visualization:** Spend 10 minutes each day visualizing your ideal AI-powered coaching business. What does it look like? How does it feel to run it?

4. **Affirmations:** Create and recite daily affirmations that reinforce your mindset mastery. For example, "I am constantly learning and growing in my use of AI to serve my clients better."

5. **Mindful Learning:** When using an AI tool, practice mindfulness. Pay attention to what you're doing, how the AI is assisting you, and how you can improve your use of it.

Overcoming Mindset Blocks

Even with the best intentions, you might encounter mindset blocks when it comes to integrating AI into your coaching practice. Here are some common blocks and how to overcome them:

1. **Fear of Obsolescence:** You might worry that AI will make your skills obsolete. Remember, AI is a tool, not a replacement. Your human skills—empathy, intuition, creativity—are more valuable than ever in the AI era.

2. **Overwhelm:** The rapid pace of AI development can feel overwhelming. Combat this by focusing on one AI tool or application at a time. Master it before moving on to the next.

3. **Imposter Syndrome:** You might feel like you're not "tech-savvy" enough to use AI effectively. Remember, everyone starts as a beginner. Give yourself permission to learn and make mistakes.

4. **Perfectionism:** You might hesitate to use AI tools because they're not perfect. Remember, perfection is the enemy of progress. It's better to start using AI imperfectly than to not start at all.

5. **Resistance to Change:** It's natural to resist change, especially if your current methods are working. But remember, what got you here won't get you there. Embrace change as an opportunity for growth.

The Seven-Figure Mindset

As you work towards your seven-figure coaching business, your mindset will be your most valuable asset. The coaches who reach this level of success are those who are constantly learning, adapting, and innovating. They see AI not as a threat, but as a powerful ally in their mission to impact more lives.

Imagine waking up each day excited about the possibilities AI brings to your coaching practice. Picture yourself confidently using AI tools to create personalized coaching experiences for your clients, to scale your business beyond what you thought possible, and to free up your time to focus on what you do best—transforming lives.

This is not just a fantasy. With the right mindset and the power of AI, it's a reality that's within your reach.

Remember, your mindset is the foundation upon which your AI-powered coaching empire will be built. Cultivate it with care, nurture it with continuous learning, and watch as it propels you to heights you've only dreamed of.

Following we'll dive into how AI can help you identify and target your perfect clients with unprecedented precision. Get ready to discover how AI can help you find your ideal niche and dominate it.

Key Takeaways:

- A growth mindset is crucial when integrating AI into your coaching practice
- Successful AI-savvy coaches continuously learn and adapt
- Overcoming mindset blocks is key to fully leveraging AI in your business

Action Steps:

1. Conduct a mindset audit. Identify any limiting beliefs you have about AI and challenge them.

2. Choose one AI tool you've been hesitant to try. Commit to learning and implementing it in your business this week.

3. Find an "AI accountability partner" - another coach who's also learning to integrate AI. Schedule weekly check-ins to share progress and challenges.

4. Create a "success log" where you record your daily wins with AI, no matter how small.

5. Identify a coach who's successfully using AI. Reach out to them for a virtual coffee chat to learn from their experience. (Note: I hope you know you found one here 😊)

Chapter 5
Perfect Client Precision: AI-Driven Avatars & Niching Down

*I*n the world of coaching, knowing your ideal client is not just important—it's everything! It's the difference between struggling to fill your roster and having a waitlist of eager clients. It's the key to creating programs that sell themselves and marketing that resonates deeply. And with AI, we can take client precision to a whole new level.

Let me share a personal story that illustrates the importance of finding your perfect niche and avatar. For the first 30 years of my career, I focused on helping entrepreneurs nurture themselves and build their businesses to six- and seven-figure incomes. But over time, I felt called to do more. I chose to serve women who were successful professionally but were in tremendous personal pain. Many would use food to feel better due to past traumas, and I was passionate about showing them a new path to nourish themselves and flourish, body and soul.

That's when I started a division of coaching called "FINE to FAB", helping successful women go from feeling F.I.N.E. (F'd Up, Insecure, Neurotic & Emotional) to feeling F.A.B. (Fabulous, Awesome, Beautiful) without years of shame, blame, or therapy.

Now, here's where it gets interesting. I didn't just jump into this niche blindly. I hired a renowned consultant to evaluate the space, investing over $30,000 to have the research done. We dug deep to learn more about my avatar, how to market to her, who else was already working with her so I could partner or joint venture, what she was consuming as far as content and where, whom she was following, where to find her, and what we needed to create to solve her biggest problem.

The result? We built that division of the business into the amazing company it is today, saving thousands of lives and making a difference. I wrote a book called "FINE to FAB", which got me on CBS, The Talk. Later, every national TV network, including ABC, NBC, FOX, CW and TEDx, invited me to share my message of hope and freedom for these women.

This experience reminded me how important it is to truly understand your avatar and niche. Know that what used to take months and an abundance of money can now be done in minutes and for free. When you understand how to use AI and make it work for you, you have the power of the world in hand. Let's get started now, shall we?

Now, let's talk about how you can find your perfect niche and ideal client avatar using AI:

1. AI-Enhanced Client Avatar Creation

Use tools like ChatGPT or Claude (free or fee version) to help define your ideal client avatar. Here's what's possible:

- Generate detailed buyer persona descriptions
- Identify pain points and desires
- Create psychographic profiles

For a more comprehensive approach, let's use the BENDWIMP framework:

AI Generated

Ideal Client Avatar

B - Behaviors: What are their typical actions and habits?

E - Emotions: What feelings drive their decisions?

N - Needs: What are their essential requirements or desires?

D - Demographics: Age, gender, location, income, education, etc.

W - Wants: What are their aspirations or wishes?

I - Interests: What topics or activities captivate them?

M - Motivations: What drives them to take action?

P - Pain Points: What problems or challenges are they facing?

Example Prompt: "Using the BENDWIMP framework, create a detailed client avatar for a business coach targeting female entrepreneurs in their 40s who want to scale their online businesses to seven figures."

2. Market Research & Niche Identification

AI can analyze vast amounts of data to help you identify profitable niches. Here are some resources and they have free versions available:

- Use Google Trends to analyze market trends
- Use Answer The Public to identify questions people are asking in your niche
- Use Ubersuggest for keyword research and content ideas

Action Step: Use Google Trends to compare interest in different coaching niches over the past year. Identify growing trends that align with your expertise.

3. AI-Powered Competitor Analysis

Understand your competition better with AI:

- Use ChatGPT to analyze competitors' websites and social media content
- Identify their unique selling propositions
- Find opportunities to differentiate yourself

Example Prompt: "Analyze the website content of [Competitor Name] and identify their main value propositions and target audience. Then, suggest three ways I could differentiate my coaching services from theirs."

4. Personalized Marketing Messages

Once you've defined your niche and avatar, use AI to create personalized marketing messages:

- Use Copy.ai or Jasper (both have free trials) to generate customized email sequences and social media posts
- Create targeted landing page copy

Example Tool: Use Copy.ai's free trial to generate 10 different email subject lines tailored to your ideal client avatar. (Note: ChatGPT/Claude/ Gemini can also do this for you.)

5. Continuous Refinement

- Use AI to continuously refine your understanding of your ideal client:
- Use ChatGPT/Claude to analyze client feedback and testimonials
- Identify patterns in successful client relationships
- Adjust your avatar and niche focus based on real-world data

Example Prompt: "I'm going to provide you with 5 client testimonials. Please analyze them and identify common themes, pain points addressed, and results achieved. Then, suggest how I might refine my ideal client avatar based on this information."

Remember: the riches are in the niches. It's about being laser-focused and narrowing it down to a specific avatar. I know you think you can help everyone, but when you don't speak to them, they don't hear your message. When you speak to a specific person, you will be heard.

We want to make sure that you narrow down your avatar and niche it down to the point where the person raises their hand and says, "Oh my goodness, you're talking to me. You know me." And that's the key thing, knowing your avatar and knowing their beliefs, their values, their rules, their pains, their behaviors, being able to serve them at the highest level to get them the outcomes that they want.

Key Take Aways:

- AI can help create detailed, data-driven client avatars
- Niching down is crucial for standing out in a crowded market
- The BENDWIMP framework helps define your ideal client

Action Steps:

1. **Use ChatGPT to create a detailed client avatar** based on the BENDWIMP framework. Compare this with your current understanding of your ideal client and note any new insights.
2. **Conduct an analysis** of your top 20% of clients using the BENDWIMP framework. What common characteristics emerge?
3. **Use Google Trends** to identify 5 growing sub-niches within your field. Evaluate each for viability and alignment with your strengths.
4. **Use Answer The Public** to find the top 10 questions people are asking in your niche. Use these insights to refine your understanding of your ideal client's pain points.
5. **Create an AI-generated visual** representation of your ideal client avatar using Midjourney or DALL-E (both have free options) and display it prominently in your workspace as a constant reminder.

By leveraging these affordable AI tools to create detailed client avatars and laser-focused niches, you're not just preparing for the future—you're creating it. As we move forward, we'll explore how to use these AI-facilitated insights to create high-ticket programs that your ideal clients can't resist. Get ready to take your coaching offerings to the next level!

Chapter 6
High-Ticket Coaching Programs

Designing Premium Coaching Offers

*H*ow often do you hear people tell you to sell programs for $7 and then up to $19 or $97 or $149 or $997? Oh, my goodness, do you realize that it takes the same energy to get there that it does to get someone to buy a $10,000 program or $20,000 or $30,000 or $40,000 or $50,000 or more?

Let me take you back to when I first discovered the power of high-ticket programs. I remember when I was younger, I was fortunate to be trained by Tom Hopkins and Zig Ziglar, and Ziglar used to say, "The only difference between a thousand and ten thousand is the zero."

Well, I agree. It's only a zero, and you'll find the person that spends a thousand and doesn't have it will be a lot more work than the person that spends ten thousand and has twenty.

The problem is, when you're majoring in the minors, you're going to get minors showing up, and then they need more time and attention. When you're selling high-ticket programs, you're going to get the people who are paying to pay attention. They're going to get even better outcomes because they're invested. They're invested in themselves and their outcomes.

I'm a big proponent of getting results and helping people get what they want, and I'd rather work and hold your hand to get what you want and charge you a little bit more, than give it away and not have people appreciate the value of what they're getting.

Here from a real case study that illustrates this point:

Dr. Terry White was selling her program's a la carte, $299, or $499 always adding additional one offs. I asked her, "What is it you're doing as a naturopathic doctor?" And she gave me all the details of the tests, studies, analysis, prescriptions, remedies, follow ups she provided and the results that she got for her patients the outcomes were amazing.

I said, "Terry, no longer sell programs for $299 or $499 and so forth. You're going to offer programs that are all inclusive for ONLY $2997, $4997, $7497 and $10,000." She listened to me, and I said, "Here's what's going to happen. They're going to pay to pay attention."

Within a month Dr. Terry had made over $45k with just a few new clients. That would have taken her 6 months to a year based on how she was valuing her time and service.

Before, they'd come in, do a test or two, and she'd be following up with them three months, six months, and so forth, not always charging for her time. She was working for pennies on the dollars and working so hard for them, but they weren't working for themselves.

Now she can offer an even better quality of care and her patients can get more of her without it affecting her business.

When we changed the way she was marketing and to whom she was marketing, the deliverables remained the same amazing service, but what happened is the results were even better. People appreciated it. They followed her guidelines. They did what she told them to do. Their health improved and she got raving fan customers who came back and referred her to more people because it was more valuable.

So high-ticket items are not just about making a lot of money. It's about helping people get the results they want and making sure they value what they're getting.

Leveraging AI in High-Ticket Program Design

AI can be a powerful ally in creating your high-ticket programs. Here's how:

1. **Market Analysis:** Use AI tools like ChatGPT to analyze market trends and identify gaps in the coaching market that your high-ticket program can fill.

2. **Content Structure:** AI can help outline your program modules and suggest content ideas based on your expertise and target audience.

3. **Pricing Strategy:** Utilize AI-supported pricing tools to analyze competitor offerings and suggest optimal price points for your high-ticket programs.

4. **Personalization:** Implement AI to create customized elements within your program, tailoring content to individual client needs.

Now, let's break down how you can create your own high-ticket program:

1. **Identify a Specific Problem:** Your program should solve a significant, pressing problem for your ideal clients. Use AI tools like ChatGPT to research and identify the most common pain points in your niche.

2. **Create a Unique Methodology:** Develop a step-by-step process or framework that sets you apart from other coaches. Use AI to help you brainstorm and structure your unique methodology.

3. **Offer Comprehensive Support:** This might include one-on-one coaching, group calls, resources, and tools. Use AI-supported platforms like Thinkific or Teachable to create and deliver your course content.

4. **Add High-Value Bonuses:** Think about what you can add that would be incredibly valuable to your clients. Maybe it's a retreat, like I did, or access to exclusive resources. Use AI tools like Canva's Magic Write to help create additional resources.

5. **Create a Compelling Offer:** Your offer should clearly communicate the transformation clients will experience and the unique value you provide. Use AI writing tools like ChatGPT, Claude AI, Copy.ai or Jasper to help craft your sales copy.

6. **Price for Profit:** Remember my story - make sure you're accounting for all costs and pricing for healthy profit margins. Use AI to help you create financial models and determine optimal pricing.

7. **Personalize the Experience:** Use the detailed avatar you created in the previous section to tailor your program to your ideal client's needs. Implement a CRM system like HubSpot CRM (free tier available) to help manage client relationships.

Real-World Success: The Power of High-Ticket Programs

Let's hear from Ally Jewel, who experienced the transformative power of high-ticket program creation:

"I worked with Lisa several years ago, and back then, it took us six months to launch my program that brought in six figures. Recently, using the power of AI and Lisa's incredible genius, we created a comprehensive marketing product launch with all the materials for my new program in just four days. The speed at which Lisa operates and implements is awe-inspiring. Her ability to know exactly what you need in the moment, how to structure it, and the steps needed to launch it is beyond my wildest dreams."

Ally's experience demonstrates how combining AI with strategic coaching can dramatically accelerate the creation and launch of high-ticket programs, leading to significant revenue growth in a fraction of the time.

Remember, shifting to high-ticket programs isn't just about charging more. It's about providing immense value and transformative results for your clients. When you do this right, everyone wins - you earn more while making a bigger impact, and your clients get life-changing results.

Key Take Aways:

- AI can help design, price, and sell high-value coaching programs
- High-ticket offerings attract committed clients and lead to better outcomes
- AI assists in creating unique methodologies and personalizing the client experience

Action Steps:

1. Use **ChatGPT to brainstorm 10 potential high-ticket program** ideas based on your expertise and ideal client's needs.
2. **Create a unique methodology** for your chosen program idea. Use AI to help you structure and name your process.
3. List out all the components of your high-ticket offer, including support, resources, and bonuses.
4. Use an AI writing tool to draft your program description and sales copy.
5. **Conduct a pricing analysis** using AI to determine the optimal price point for your program.

As you implement these steps, remember that your high-ticket program is a reflection of your unique value and expertise. It's time to ensure that your brand aligns perfectly with the premium offer you've just created. Let's explore how AI can help you craft a brand identity that's as compelling as your new high-ticket program.

Chapter 7
Branding Brilliance:
Crafting Your Identity with AI

*I*n today's crowded coaching market, having a strong, distinctive brand isn't just nice to have—it's essential. Your brand is more than just a logo or a color scheme; it's the total experience of working with you. It's what sets you apart and makes you memorable. And with AI, we can take your branding to a whole new level.

Let me share a quick story. When I first started FINE to FAB, I struggled with whether to run my coaching business as "FINE to FAB" or as "Lisa Lieberman-Wang". I examined dozens of people in the same field of "Business & Life Strategist", with Tony Robbins coming out on top. I recall his going to franchise his firm, only to have to buy it back from the buyers after it failed. People wanted him because the company's name included his name.

I evaluated this case study and concluded that I would make the company name the product name, so that my personal name would not be attached to it. It sounded like a good plan at the time.

FINE TO FAB, the book I wrote, became a number one best seller, selling thousands of copies. I ended up on CBS, The Talk, and Curvy Girls, a reality show. Then I was a regular on television on all the stations, began speaking for large corporations, spoke at the Navy, at Harvard, and was offered an opportunity to do a TEDx Talk. I continued to promote FINE to FAB, and they continued to promote Lisa Lieberman-Wang (LLW). I recognized they each have a purpose, and I needed to make LLW more obvious.

Today, I advertise LLW and have three products under my name: FINE to FAB, Mastery to Millions Mastermind, and Platinum Business Coaching.

The lesson? Your brand evolves, and it's crucial to be adaptable while maintaining a strong core identity.

Now, let's dive into how AI can help you create a powerful brand:

1. Brand Voice and Messaging

AI Application: Use ChatGPT or Claude to help define your brand voice. **Prompt example:** "Based on my coaching niche of [your niche] and my target audience of [your avatar description], help me create a brand voice guide including tone, vocabulary, and key messaging points."

2. Visual Identity

AI Application: Use Midjourney, DALL-E, or Ideogram to generate visual concepts for your brand. **Prompt example:** "Create a modern, professional logo concept for a life coaching business focused on empowering women in their careers. Use warm, inspiring colors."

3. Color Psychology

AI Application: Use ChatGPT to understand color psychology for your brand. **Prompt example:** "Explain the psychological effects and brand associations of the colors blue, green, and orange in the context of a personal development coaching brand."

4. Brand Story

AI Application: Use GPT-4 or Claude to help craft your brand story. **Prompt example:** "Help me create a compelling brand story for my coaching business. Include my background as [brief background], my passion for [your passion], and how I help clients [main benefit you provide]."

5. Competitor Analysis

AI Application: Use tools like SEMrush or Ahrefs (which have AI components) to analyze competitor brands. **Action:** Input your top competitors into these tools and analyze their brand positioning, messaging, and visual elements.

6. Brand Consistency

AI Application: Use Canva's Magic Write feature to create on-brand social media posts. **Prompt example:** In Canva, use Magic Write and input "Create 5 Instagram post captions that align with my brand voice as a [your niche] coach, focusing on [key brand message]."

7. Brand Personality

AI Application: Use ChatGPT to define your brand personality. **Prompt example:** "Based on the archetypes of Hero, Sage, Explorer, and Caregiver, help me determine which best fits my coaching brand and why. My coaching focuses on [brief description of your coaching]."

Real-World Success: AI-Powered Rebranding

Let's look at how a coach successfully used AI to enhance their brand:

Joanna, a Wellness Coach, was struggling to stand out in a saturated market. She turned to AI tools to revamp her brand identity and saw remarkable results. Joanna used Midjourney to generate a unique logo that embodied health and vitality, ChatGPT to craft a compelling brand story that resonated with her mission, and Copy.ai to create consistent messaging across her platforms.

The result? After her AI-assisted rebrand, Joanna noticed significant improvements. Her new brand resonated strongly with her target audience, leading to increased website traffic and more client inquiries. Her social media following grew, and she received invitations to speak at wellness conferences, highlighting her enhanced industry presence.

"AI didn't just help me create a brand," Joanna says. "It helped me articulate my unique value proposition clearly and effectively, something I struggled with before."

AI Tool Recommendations for Branding

Here's a quick reference guide for AI branding tools:

Branding Aspect	AI Tool	Key Feature
Voice & Messaging	ChatGPT/ Claude AI	Natural language generation
Visual Identity	DALL-E, Midjourney, or Ideogram	Image generation from text descriptions
Color Psychology	Adobe Color	AI-powered color wheel and palettes
Brand Story	GPT-4 or Claude	Advanced language model for narrative creation
Competitor Analysis	SEMrush	AI-driven market analysis
Brand Consistency	Canva's Magic Write	AI-assisted design and content creation
Brand Personality	Crystal	AI personality insights

Measuring Brand Impact with AI

To truly understand the effectiveness of your branding efforts, leverage AI-driven analytics tools. Platforms like Brandwatch use AI to analyze social media mentions, sentiment, and engagement. Google Analytics 4 employs machine learning to provide deeper insights into user behavior on your website.

Set up these tools to track key metrics like brand mentions, sentiment, website traffic, and conversion rates. AI can help you identify trends and patterns, allowing you to refine your branding strategy continually.

Maintaining Brand Authenticity with AI

While AI is a powerful tool, it's crucial to maintain your authentic voice. Use AI as a starting point or for inspiration, but always infuse your unique personality and experiences into your brand. Remember, your clients are choosing to work with you, not an AI.

A good practice is to use AI to generate ideas or first drafts, then personally review and refine the content to ensure it truly reflects your voice and values.

Adapting Your Brand Across Platforms

Different social media platforms have distinct audiences and content styles. Use AI to help you adapt your brand for each platform while maintaining consistency.

For instance, you might use ChatGPT to help you transform a long-form LinkedIn article into a series of punchy posts or engaging captions for Instagram posts. Hootsuite's or Later AI-powered tools can help you optimize posting times for each platform, ensuring maximum engagement.

Remember, while AI can provide incredible insights and assist in creating elements of your brand, the essence of your brand should come from you. Your unique experiences, philosophy, and approach are what truly make your brand special.

Key Take Aways:

- AI tools can help develop a unique and consistent brand identity
- Your brand should evolve while maintaining a strong core identity
- AI can assist in analyzing competitor brands and optimizing your brand positioning
- Measure your brand impact using AI-fueled analytics tools
- Maintain authenticity by using AI as a tool, not a replacement for your unique voice

Action Steps:

1. **Use ChatGPT or Claude to create your brand voice guide.** Prompt: "Create a brand voice guide for my coaching business, focusing on [your niche]. Include tone, key phrases, and words to avoid."

2. **Generate logo concepts** using Midjourney, DALL-E or Ideogram. Prompt: "Create a logo for a coaching business named [your business name] that focuses on [your niche]. Use colors that evoke [emotions you want to evoke]."

3. **Use SEMrush or Ahrefs to analyze** your top 3 competitors' branding. Look for gaps in the market that you can fill with your unique brand positioning.

4. **Craft your brand story using GPT-4 or Claude.** Prompt: "Help me write a 300-word brand story for my coaching business. Include my background as [your background], my passion for [your passion], and how I help clients [main benefit you provide]."

5. **Create a week's worth of on-brand social media** content using Canva's Magic Write. Prompt: "Create 7 social media post ideas for a [your niche] coach, focusing on [key brand message]. Include a mix of inspirational quotes, tips, and client success stories."

6. **Set up AI-powered analytics tools** like Google Analytics 4 to track your brand's performance across different platforms.

With your brand identity solidified, you're now ready to attract your ideal clients like never before. It's time to dive into creating a marketing strategy that aligns perfectly with your new, powerhouse brand.

Chapter 8
Marketing Magic: AI Strategies for Explosive Lead Generation

*W*elcome to the game-changing strategies that will revolutionize how you attract high-ticket clients. We're about to dive into the world of AI-powered marketing strategies that will have your ideal clients lining up to work with you. But before we explore these cutting-edge techniques, let me share a personal story that illustrates the power of smart marketing.

When I launched Mastery to Millions, I faced a significant challenge. My previous program, FINE to FAB, catered primarily to professional women dealing with personal struggles. Now, I needed to reach a completely different demographic: coaches, consultants, and entrepreneurs looking to scale their businesses to seven figures.

This shift meant I couldn't rely solely on my existing network. That's when I fully embraced two powerful concepts: "OPP" (Other People's People) and "OPS" (Other People's Stages).

I reached out to influencers, business leaders, and organizations that already had my new ideal clients in their audience. By partnering with them and offering to speak on their platforms about business growth and AI-driven strategies, I tapped into a whole new market virtually overnight.

For instance, I collaborated with the founder of B.I.G - Believe Inspire Grow. To date, Tara has more than 10,000 women who have embraced their B.I.G. mission to continuously support and empower each other. I was invited in to help her entrepreneurs grow. This partnership not only boosted my credibility in the business coaching space but also introduced me to a vast network of entrepreneurs eager to scale their businesses.

Now, imagine supercharging this approach with AI. That's exactly what we're going to explore here. We'll dive into powerful strategies that combine cutting-edge AI tools with proven marketing techniques to help you generate a flood of high-quality leads for your coaching business.

Let's start with a recent case study that demonstrates the power of these strategies in action.

Case Study: "How to Build a 7-Figure Coaching Business" Book Launch

I recently launched my book, "How to Build a 7 Figure Coaching Business - Bonus Using AI: A Proven Blueprint for Getting High-Ticket Coaching Clients." Instead of going the traditional route, I leveraged AI to create a highly effective funnel:

1. **Free eBook Offer:** I offered the eBook version for free at www.howtobuilda7figurecoachingbusiness.com This allowed me to capture leads and provide immediate value.

2. **Low-Cost Physical Book:** For those who preferred a hard copy, I offered it for just the cost of shipping and handling - $7.97. This low barrier offers increased conversions.

3. **AI-generated Upsell:** Using AI, I created a sophisticated upsell sequence. The main offer was my "7 Days to Create Your 7-Figure Talk That Sells" program.

This funnel was supercharged by AI in several ways:

AI-generated copy: I used GPT-3 (now we have GPT-4o) to help craft compelling copy for each stage of the funnel, from the initial offer to the upsell pages.

Personalized email sequences: AI-generated email marketing tools helped create personalized follow-up sequences based on user behavior.

The result? Not only did we distribute thousands of books, but we also generated significant revenue from the upsell offer.

Today I would add - **Chatbot support:** An AI chatbot answered common questions about the book and the upsell offer, improving conversion rates.

Platforms like MobileMonkey, Chatfuel, and ManyChat allow you to build sophisticated chatbots that can engage with your audience 24/7, qualify leads, and even make sales while you sleep.

Challenges to Get People Engaged

Prior to this, I created a 7-day challenge called **"7 Days to Mastering A 7-Figure Signature Talk That Sells."** (the OTO, One Time Offer, I used in my book funnel). This challenge served as both a value-packed training and a lead-generation tool for my high-ticket coaching programs.

Here's how we structured the challenge:

- Day 1: Picking a Topic That Sells
- Day 2: Attracting Your Audience
- Day 3: Mastering a Signature Talk That Sells
- Day 4: Building Your Brand & Product/Solution
- Day 5: Call to Action & What Makes Them Say "Yes"
- Day 6: Delivery Methods
- Day 7: How to Get on Stages

We did this challenge, "old school" prior to AI.

Now this is how you can do it with AI to enhance every aspect of this challenge:

1. **Content Creation:** AI writing tools will help you outline and draft content for each day, ensuring each session is packed with value.

   Tools like ChatGPT, Claude AI, Copy Ai, Jasper AI can generate high-quality copy across various styles and tones, perfect for creating diverse content for your marketing campaigns.

   For visual content, Lexica Art can produce realistic AI-generated images for blog thumbnails and social media posts, enhancing your visual marketing strategy.

2. **Personalized Learning Paths:** AI-supported learning management systems create tailored experiences based on participant progress and engagement.

   Engagement Boosting: AI chatbots and automated messaging kept participants engaged throughout the challenge. Today you can put your social media on steroids with Mobile Monkey and Many Chat responding as you and creating real engagement.

3. **Real-Time Analytics:** AI-driven analytics tools will help track participant engagement, allowing us to adjust content and delivery in real-time.

4. **Automated Follow-Up:** After the challenge, AI-powered email sequences nurtured leads towards our high-ticket offers.

   The results were staggering each time we rolled out this funnel they generated hundreds of thousands of dollars in new revenue, even hitting the seven-figure mark when including subsequent high-ticket sales.

Now, let's break down the key AI-powered strategies you can implement in your own coaching business:

1. AI-Enhanced Content Creation

Use tools like GPT-4o, Claude, Jasper, or Copy.ai to help generate ideas, outlines, and even first drafts of your content. This can include blog posts, social media content, email sequences, and more.

> **Action Step:** Use this prompt in ChatGPT: "Create a content plan for a 30-day social media campaign promoting a high-ticket coaching program for [your niche]. Include post ideas, hashtags, and call-to-action suggestions."

2. Personalized Email Marketing

Implement AI-powered email marketing tools like Active Campaign to optimize send times and personalize content based on subscriber behavior.

> **Action Step:** Set up an A/B test for your next email campaign using AI-generated subject lines and analyze the results.

3. AI-Powered Chatbots

Use tools like MobileMonkey or ManyChat to create sophisticated chatbots that can qualify leads, answer questions, and guide potential clients toward your offers 24/7.

> **Action Step:** Design a chatbot flow using this prompt in ChatGPT: "Create a conversation flow for a chatbot that qualifies leads for a high-ticket coaching program. Include questions about business size, current challenges, growth goals, and budget range."

4. Video Marketing with AI

Leverage AI tools like Synthesia, Invideo, Vidyo AI and Descript to create engaging video content quickly and at scale.

> **Action Step:** Use an AI video creation tool to transform your best-performing blog post into a short, engaging video for social media.

5. AI-Driven Advertising

Use platforms like Albert.ai or Adext AI to optimize your ad campaigns, from audience targeting to ad creative selection.

> **Action Step:** Set up a small test campaign using an AI advertising platform and compare its performance to your manually managed campaigns.

6. Predictive Analytics

Implement AI-powered analytics tools to predict which leads are most likely to convert, allowing you to focus your efforts more effectively.

Action Step: Research predictive analytics tools that integrate with your current CRM or marketing automation platform.

7. AI-Enhanced Funnel Optimization

Use AI to continuously test and optimize each stage of your marketing funnel, from lead magnets to high-ticket offer.

Action Step: Use this prompt in ChatGPT: "Suggest 5 ways to optimize a marketing funnel for a high-ticket coaching program, focusing on the transition from free content to paid offer."

Remember, the goal of using AI in your marketing is not to remove the human element but to enhance it. AI should free you up to do more of what you do best – connecting with clients, delivering transformative coaching, and growing your business.

By implementing these AI-supported strategies, you're positioning yourself at the forefront of the coaching industry. You're leveraging technology to reach more people, provide more value, and ultimately, make a bigger impact while growing your business to seven figures and beyond.

NOTE: All actions steps were positioned throughout this chapter. Go back and make sure you apply what you are learning.

Real-World Success: Transforming Paid Talks into Five-Figure Sales

Roya, an intuitive healer and certified coach, experienced firsthand the transformative power of combining AI with proven marketing strategies. Through her work with me, Roya learned to harness AI to elevate her business and serve more clients at a higher level.

"Lisa has been an extraordinary mentor in transforming how I convert audiences into loyal clients. Through her Million Dollar Close technique, she taught me to communicate more succinctly and powerfully with my ideal avatar, making them feel truly understood and connected.

With Lisa's guidance, I identified my ideal client avatar and used AI to craft communications that speak directly to their needs and desires. Lisa helped me develop scripts using AI, making every interaction feel personal and resonant, as if I truly knew them in their soul.

Her Mastery to Millions methodology turned my paid talks into additional five-figure sales multiple times. By following her proven strategies, I have significantly increased my client base and now serve even more people at a higher level.

Lisa continues to introduce me to advanced AI tools that streamline my work, allowing me to focus on what I do best – transforming lives. Her deep knowledge, innovative approach, and unwavering support have made a profound impact on my business. I highly recommend Lisa to anyone looking to elevate their business and achieve outstanding results."

Next we'll explore how to use AI to create high-converting sales funnels that seamlessly guide your leads from initial interest to becoming high-ticket clients. Get ready to transform your sales process!

Key Take Aways:

- AI enhances marketing strategies across multiple channels
- Personalization at scale becomes possible with AI-powered marketing
- AI helps in creating and optimizing marketing funnels

Chapter 9
High-Converting Funnels: Designing Sales Funnels That Sell

Come with me: You're at a networking event, and you spot someone who's the perfect fit for your coaching program. You wouldn't immediately pitch your $10,000 package, would you? Of course not. You'd start a conversation, build rapport, offer value, and guide them toward seeing how you could help them. That's exactly what a well-designed sales funnel does, but at scale and with the power of AI.

Imagine the potential of a well-structured AI-powered sales funnel for a health coach struggling to fill their programs. Let's explore what's possible with the right strategies and tools.

Suppose he/she wants to attract more clients and streamline their marketing efforts. They could start with a free webinar on "5 Secrets to Lasting Weight Loss." AI can assist in crafting a compelling title and optimizing the landing page copy to maximize sign-ups. After the webinar, the real magic happens with an AI-supported follow-up system.

An AI-driven email sequence can nurture attendees based on their behavior during the webinar. Those who watched the entire session might receive one set of emails, while those who left early might get different content. The AI analyzes open rates, click-throughs, and even the time of day each person tends to engage with emails, tailoring the communication to everyone's preferences.

For highly engaged attendees, an AI chatbot could invite them to book a call with the coach. This chatbot can answer common questions, provide additional information about the coach's approach, and even handle basic objections.

The result? With an AI-powered funnel, a coach could see their program fill rate soar. AI's ability to personalize interactions and provide timely follow-ups can transform a scattered marketing effort into a highly effective, automated process.

Now, let's break down the key elements of a high-converting funnel and how AI can supercharge each step:

1. Irresistible Lead Magnet

Your funnel starts with attracting the right people. This could be a webinar, eBook, quiz, or video series. The key is to offer something your ideal client desperately wants.

AI can help you identify trends in your niche and even generate ideas for lead magnets. It can write compelling titles and help create the content itself.

2. Landing Pages That Convert

Once you have your lead magnet, you need a landing page that converts visitors into leads. AI can analyze thousands of high-performing landing pages and help you craft copy that resonates with your audience.

I once worked with a coach whose landing page had a 15% opt-in rate. After using AI to optimize the headline, sub headlines, and call-to-action, that rate shot up to 45%. That's triple the leads from the same traffic!

> **Tool Spotlight:** Headlime is an AI-powered tool that creates optimized landing page copy. It analyzes your input and generates compelling headlines, body text, and calls-to-action that resonate with your target audience. This tool can significantly improve your landing page conversion rates.

3. Nurture Sequences That Build Relationships

After someone opts in, the nurturing begins. This is usually done through email, but can also include retargeting ads, SMS, or even direct mail. The goal is to build a relationship and gently guide the lead towards your offer. AI can personalize these sequences in ways that were impossible just a few years ago. It can analyze a lead's behavior and adjust the content, timing, and even tone of your messages accordingly.

> **Tool Spotlight:** Reply.io uses AI to automate email responses and engagement for sales campaigns. It can analyze the best times to send emails and even adjust the content based on recipient behavior, making your nurture sequences more effective and personalized.

4. Chatbots That Qualify Leads

Imagine having a sales assistant who works 24/7, qualifying leads while you sleep. That's the power of AI-operated chatbots. They can engage visitors, answer questions, and even book sales calls.

Tool Spotlight: MobileMonkey and ManyChat allow you to create sophisticated chatbots for platforms like Facebook Messenger. These bots can engage visitors, answer questions, and even book sales calls, effectively qualifying leads 24/7.

5. Sales Conversations That Close

At some point, you'll invite your lead to have a sales conversation. AI can help prep for these conversations by providing insights about the lead and even suggesting talking points.

I've seen coaches increase their close rates by 50% or more by using AI to prep for sales calls. It's like having a super-smart assistant whispering insights in your ear.

Here from a real case study:

"Lisa's AI-supported strategies have been a game-changer for our coaching business. As a platinum business coaching client, I've seen firsthand how she transforms abstract ideas into high-converting funnels with remarkable results.

With Lisa's guidance, we built a robust relationship coaching practice, leveraging cutting-edge AI tools to develop our entire funnel - from our website and landing pages to content, blogs, and social media presence. The transformation was extraordinary; our online presence became significantly more impactful and engaging, driving a steady stream of high-quality leads.

But the real magic happened when we implemented her '7-Figure Talk That Sells' strategy. Using AI-optimized scripts and marketing materials, each talk we delivered generated five figures. The funnel Lisa helped us create, from initial contact to high-ticket sales, worked like a well-oiled machine.

What's more, Lisa applied these same AI-produced funnel strategies to our Airbnb in Puerto Rico, maximizing our reach and retention. Her ability to use AI to generate captivating content that attracts and retains clients across different business models is truly exceptional.

Thanks to Lisa's AI-enhanced approach, we've seen a dramatic increase in our client base and revenue. For anyone looking to create high-converting funnels and achieve extraordinary results, Lisa's AI strategies are the secret weapon you need."

– Frankie,
Relationship Coach and Hacienda Serena,
PR Airbnb Owner

6. Upsells and Cross-sells That Maximize Value

Once someone becomes a client, the funnel doesn't end. AI can analyze client behavior and suggest relevant upsells or cross-sells, increasing the lifetime value of each client.

One coach I worked with implemented AI upsell recommendations and saw her average client value increase by 30% almost overnight.

> **Tool Spotlight:** While not specifically for coaches, tools like Albert.ai can be adapted for coaching services. Albert uses AI to optimize digital ad campaigns, which can be used to promote upsells and cross-sells to your existing clients.

7. Personalized Video Messages

Nothing builds trust like face-to-face interaction. AI can help you scale this personal touch by creating personalized video messages at scale.

> **Tool Spotlight:** Descript, while primarily a video editing tool, has AI-produced features that can help you create and personalize video content at scale. Its text-based editing and audio transcription features can save you significant time in creating personalized video messages.

Remember, a great funnel feels less like a sales pitch and more like a helpful friend guiding someone towards a solution they need. AI helps you be that friend to thousands of people simultaneously.

Key Take Aways:

- AI can optimize each stage of your sales funnel
- Personalization and automation are key to high-converting funnels
- AI assists in creating compelling content and analyzing funnel performance

Action Steps:

1. Analyze your current funnel using an AI tool. Look for drop-off points and opportunities for optimization.
2. Use an AI writing assistant to craft 5 different headlines for your lead magnet. Test them with a small audience to see which performs best.
3. Implement an AI-powered chatbot on your landing page. Train it to answer the top 10 questions your prospects usually ask.
4. Set up an AI-driven email sequence that adapts based on subscriber behavior. Start with three different paths based on engagement levels.

5. Use an AI tool to analyze your sales calls. Look for patterns in objections and create a script to address the top 3 most common concerns.

As we continue our journey into AI-driven coaching, we'll explore how to use AI to keep your clients engaged and coming back for more. After all, acquiring a new client is great, but retaining them is where the real magic happens.

Chapter 10
Seamless Communication: Automating Client Engagement

*P*icture this: It's 2 AM, and one of your clients is having a breakthrough moment. They're excited, inspired, and have a burning question. In the past, they'd have to wait until morning, potentially losing that spark of motivation. But what if you could be there for them, right at that moment, without sacrificing your own sleep or sanity?

This isn't a far-fetched dream. It's the reality that AI-driven communication tools are creating for coaches like us. I bet many of you can relate to the struggle of being fantastic at helping clients but drowning in a sea of emails, check-ins, and schedule juggling. You became a coach to transform lives, not to be chained to your inbox, right?

Well, here's how YOU can turn things around using AI:

1. Personalized Email Campaigns That Feel Human

We've all received those generic, robotic emails that make us feel like just another number. That's not what we're talking about here.

You can use Jasper or Copy AI to craft email sequences that feel like you've written them personally for each client. The AI will analyze each client's behavior - what emails they open, what links they click, even what time of day they engage most.

For instance, if a client is working on their resume, they'll get tips and encouragement specifically about that. If they're preparing for interviews, the emails will focus on interview strategies.

The result? You could see your email open rates skyrocket from 22% to 78% or even higher. But more importantly, you'll start getting replies like, "Wow, it's like you read my mind! This is exactly what I needed today."

2. A 24/7 Coaching Assistant (That Doesn't Need Sleep)

Remember that 2 AM scenario? Here's where it gets exciting.

You can set up a MobileMonkey or ManyChat chatbot on your website and Facebook page. But this won't be your average "How may I help you?" bot. This one will understand complex queries and provide genuinely helpful responses.

Imagine a client asking about salary negotiation strategies in the middle of the night. Your bot could provide a thoughtful answer, share a relevant resource, and even schedule a follow-up call with you if needed.

You might soon hear a client say, "I was nervous about an interview and couldn't sleep. Your bot gave me some great last-minute tips that really boosted my confidence. I nailed the interview!"

3. Smart Scheduling That Respects Everyone's Time

We've all played the "When are you free?" email tennis. It's frustrating and time-consuming. You can integrate Zapier with your scheduling system to create an AI-like automation that learns from each interaction.

If a client consistently reschedules morning appointments, the system will start suggesting afternoon slots instead. It can even factor in your energy levels, ensuring you have breaks between intense sessions.

You might hear a client remark, "I don't know how you do it, but you always seem to suggest the perfect time slot for me!"

4. Personalized Content That Keeps Them Engaged

Using Content at Scale, you can create a system that recommends relevant content to each client based on their stage in your coaching program and individual goals.

If a client is working on their personal brand, for example, the system might suggest your blog post on LinkedIn profile optimization. It'll track which recommendations each client engages with and use this data to improve future suggestions.

You might start hearing things like, "It's uncanny how you always seem to know exactly what I need to learn next!"

The impact of these changes can be profound. You could potentially take on 50% more clients while reducing your working hours. Your client satisfaction scores could soar, and your retention rate might improve by 40% or more.

But here's the kicker: Despite all this automation, your clients will likely report feeling more personally supported than ever. **The AI won't replace your human touch -- it'll enhance it.** It'll handle the routine stuff, freeing you to have deeper, more meaningful interactions with your clients when it really matters.

That's the true power of AI-driven communication. It's not about replacing human interaction, but about being there for your clients in a more personal, consistent, and helpful way than ever before.

Let me share a quick success story. One of our coaches I'll call her Sue, implemented these AI-generated ROI communication strategies in her business coaching practice. Within three months, she saw remarkable results:

- Her client retention rate increased
- She was able to take on even more clients without increasing her work hours
- She saved an average of 15 hours per week on routine communication tasks

Sue says, "The AI tools allowed me to be there for my clients in ways I never could before. I'm providing more value, and my clients feel more supported than ever. It's a win-win!"

Now, I can almost hear you thinking, "This sounds great, but I'm not tech-savvy. Can I really do this?" The answer is a resounding yes! Start small, experiment, and build from there. Here's how you can get started:

Key Take Aways:

- AI tools can automate and personalize client communications
- Chatbots and AI-designed email sequences enhance client engagement
- AI helps maintain consistent communication while freeing up your time

Action Steps:

1. Audit your current client communication process. What takes up most of your time? What do clients always ask about? These are prime candidates for AI automation.

2. Sign up for a free trial of Jasper or Copy AI. Create a template for a personalized check-in email. Test it with a small group of clients and ask for their feedback.

3. Install a MobileMonkey or ManyChat chatbot on your website. Start by programming it to handle your top 3 most common client queries. Add more over time as you see what questions come up most often.

4. Set up a Google Alert for your clients' names or companies. It's a simple way to stay on top of their achievements or challenges without fancy AI (yet!).

Remember, the goal isn't to remove yourself from the equation. It's to free you up to do more of what you do best -- coaching and transforming lives. Start small, stay curious, and watch as your practice transforms into a more efficient, effective, and personally fulfilling endeavor.

Your future self (and your clients) will thank you!

Implementation Tips

To help you implement these strategies smoothly:

1. **Start with one AI tool at a time.** Master it before moving on to the next.

2. **Involve your clients** in the process. Ask for their feedback on AI-generated communications.

3. **Regularly review and refine your AI systems.** What worked last month might need tweaking this month.

4. **Don't forget the human touch.** Use the time AI saves you to deepen your personal connections with clients.

5. **Stay informed about new AI developments** in coaching. The field is evolving rapidly, and new tools are constantly emerging.

Chapter 11
Content Creation Unleashed: AI Tools for Engaging Media

Gone are the days of writing your own content, thinking up a topic, creating it and spending four or five hours on one blog. How exciting to know that once we do the foundational work and we have AI get to know our voice, our services, our product, our avatar, our ideal client, their needs, their wants, their desires, we can, in a blink of an eye, ask it to create blog topics for us to refine those to be even more personal to what they really want and need.

We can have it research SEO for what people are actually looking for and make sure the titles are juicy and hot and will actually get people to want to go read it and spend time on your website. We can also have it help us create the social media content. We can have it write the scripts for your video. We can have it take it to the whole next level.

AI today is so huge that if you don't even want to do the videos, we can use services like HeyGen and have you record yourself and have your face up there and then record your voice and give it a script and we can have them done for you and you don't even have to do it anymore but we can have a VA feed it into HeyGen and have all these videos done.

So, AI has revolutionized the way we can create engaging video and there's so many apps and software applications available to us today to make them stand out and be dazzling.

Let's break down some key areas where AI can supercharge your content creation:

Written Content

Tools like ChatGPT and Claude can help you:

- Generate blog post ideas and outlines
- Write full articles or drafts
- Create email newsletters
- Develop course materials and worksheets

Prompt example: "Create an outline for a blog post titled '5 Ways AI is Revolutionizing Coaching Businesses in 2024'. Include an introduction, 5 main points with subpoints, and a conclusion."

Social Media Content

Use tools like Copy.ai or Jasper to:

- Generate a month's worth of social media posts
- Create platform-specific content (LinkedIn, Instagram, Twitter)
- Develop hashtag strategies
- Write engaging bios and about sections

Prompt example: "Generate 10 Instagram post ideas about the benefits of AI in coaching. Each post should be under 280 characters and include a relevant hashtag."

Video Content

Tools like InVideo, Descript, Vidyo and VEED can help you:

- Turn blog posts into engaging videos
- Edit videos by editing text
- Remove filler words automatically
- Add captions and transcripts
- Create animated text overlays
- Resize videos for different social media platforms

Action step: Take your most popular blog post and use InVideo to turn it into a 2-minute video summary for social media.

AI-Generated Voices

With tools like Eleven Labs, you can:

- Create voiceovers for your videos without hiring a voice actor
- Develop multilingual content
- Create personalized audio messages for clients
- Narrate your blog posts for a podcast version

Prompt example: "Generate a warm, professional male voice to narrate the following script about the importance of mindset in achieving business goals..."

AI-Supported Video Presenters

Using HeyGen or Synthesia, you can:

- Create a virtual you to deliver content when you're unavailable
- Develop a series of educational videos with multiple AI presenters
- Create personalized welcome videos for new clients
- Translate your videos into multiple languages with localized presenters

Action step: Use HeyGen to create a welcome video for your coaching program in three different languages.

Remember, the key to successful AI-generated content creation is to maintain your unique voice and expertise. AI is a tool to amplify your message, not replace it. Always review and refine the AI-generated content to ensure it aligns with your brand and provides real value to your audience.

Practical Exercises:

1. **Take your signature talk that sells** and input it into ChatGPT. Ask it to create 10 blog post ideas based on the content.
2. **Bonus:** Get Your Free Copy of my #1 Bestseller www. HowtoBuilda7FigureCoachingBusiness.com and learn about the Signature Talk That Sells.
3. **Use Copy.ai** to generate a week's worth of social media posts based on your core coaching philosophy.
4. **Use Descript** to edit your latest video coaching session into three short, value-packed clips for social media.
5. **Create a personalized welcome** message for new clients using Eleven Labs' voice generation technology.
6. **Use HeyGen to create a video** series introducing the key concepts of your coaching program.

It is worth noting that as I add more resources, I am aware that there are many others that are interchangeable and can accomplish the same task. You will discover what best meets your needs as you get to know them. You don't need them all; just the ones that work for you.

By leveraging these AI tools, you can create a content machine that consistently delivers value to your audience, positions you as an expert, and attracts high-ticket clients to your coaching business. The future of content creation is here – embrace it and watch your influence grow!

Practical Exercises: Planning Your AI-Driven Content Calendar

Creating a content calendar helps you stay organized and ensures a steady flow of content to engage your audience. Here's a step-by-step guide using AI tools.

Define Your Themes

Identify key themes for each month based on your business goals and client interests.

Example Prompt: "ChatGPT, suggest monthly content themes for my coaching business focused on financial independence, effective marketing, and personal growth."

Generate Weekly Content Ideas

Use AI to brainstorm blog post titles, social media topics, and video ideas.

Example Prompt: "Generate weekly blog post ideas and social media topics for a month, aligned with my monthly themes."

Create a Detailed Content Plan

Develop a plan outlining the specific content pieces for each day of the week.

Example Prompt: "Help me create a detailed weekly content plan for my coaching business, including blog posts, social media posts, and video content."

Automate Content Distribution

Use scheduling tools to automate the publishing of your content.

Example Prompt: "Set up a content distribution schedule on Hootsuite for my upcoming blog posts and social media content."

Key Take Aways:

- AI streamlines the content creation process across various formats
- AI tools help in generating ideas, writing, and optimizing content
- Maintaining your unique voice while leveraging AI is crucial

Action Steps:

1. **Choose three AI tools -** one for writing, one for video, and one for audio. Sign up for free trials.
2. **Use these tools to create a multi-format** content piece: a blog post, a video summary, and an audio version.
3. **Share this content** with your audience and monitor engagement across formats.
4. **Ask for feedback** from trusted clients or colleagues on the AI-assisted content.
5. **Based on results and feedback, create a plan** to incorporate AI into your regular content creation process, focusing on the formats that resonate most with your audience.

Chapter 12
Unleashing The Power of AI: Your Custom GPT - AI Genius Marketing Coach

As we've journeyed through the transformative power of AI in coaching, you've learned about various tools and strategies to elevate your business.

Now, let me introduce you to a game-changer that's going to revolutionize your coaching practice: the **"AI Genius Marketing Coach - Content Planner"**. This isn't just another tool; it's like having a marketing genius and a content wizard working for you 24/7.

Remember when we talked about creating a board of advisors? Well, this is like having that board, plus a team of expert marketers and content creators, all rolled into one powerful AI assistant. I created it following the best practices I've described to you here in the book. You now will be able to plug your information in and make it sing and dance for you.

Let me break it down for you in a way that'll get you as excited as I am about this:

Know Your Clients Like Never Before

Imagine having an AI that can dig deep into your ideal client's mind. We're talking about understanding their hopes, dreams, fears, and what makes them tick. This tool doesn't just give you basic demographics; it paints a vivid picture of your client avatar that's so detailed, you'll feel like you can reach out and shake their hand.

> **Example:** Ask the AI, "Create a detailed client avatar for a life coach specializing in career transitions for women in their 40s." The response will provide insights you might never have considered.

Marketing Messages That Hit Home

Gone are the days of generic marketing that falls flat. This AI genius crafts messages that speak directly to your ideal clients' hearts. It's like having a mind-reader who knows exactly what words will make your audience sit up and take notice.

> **Example:** Prompt the AI with, "Write a compelling email subject line for a webinar on overcoming imposter syndrome in corporate leadership." You'll get multiple options that resonate with your target audience.

Content Creation on Steroids

Writer's block? That's so yesterday. This AI powerhouse churns out engaging content faster than you can say "blog post." We're talking attention-grabbing headlines, meaty articles, and social media posts that'll have your followers hitting that share button like there's no tomorrow.

> **Example:** Ask for "5 blog post ideas about mindfulness for busy entrepreneurs, including outlines for each." Within seconds, you'll have a month's worth of content planned out.

Coaching Programs That Sell Themselves

Designing your next coaching program just got a whole lot easier. The AI helps you structure your modules and exercises in a way that not only delivers results but keeps your clients coming back for more. It's like having a master architect for your coaching programs.

> **Example:** Input "Create a 6-week program outline for a group coaching program on financial wellness for millennials." The AI will provide a structured program with weekly themes and exercise ideas.

Client Relationships That Go Deep

It's not just about getting clients; it's about keeping them. This AI helps you craft personalized communication that makes each client feel like they're your only client. It's the secret sauce to building lasting relationships and a rock-solid reputation.

> **Example:** Use the prompt, "Generate a personalized check-in email template for a client who's halfway through a 3-month coaching program." The AI will create a template that you can easily customize for each client.

Data-Driven Success

No more guessing games about what's working and what's not. This AI crunches the numbers and gives you insights that'll make you feel like a business psychic. You'll know exactly what tweaks to make to skyrocket your success.

> **Example:** Ask, "What metrics should I track to measure the success of my email marketing campaigns?" The AI will provide a list of key performance indicators and explain why each is important.

Stay Ahead of the Curve

In the fast-paced world of coaching, staying innovative is key. This AI keeps you on the cutting edge, helping you experiment with fresh ideas that'll make your competitors wonder what your secret is.

> **Example:** Prompt the AI with, "Suggest three innovative ways to use augmented reality in a leadership coaching program." You'll get cutting-edge ideas to set your coaching practice apart.

Now, you might be thinking, "Lisa, this sounds too good to be true." But let me tell you, I've seen the magic this AI can work. It's like having a marketing department, a content team, and a business strategist all rolled into one, working tirelessly to help you succeed.

Case Study: The AI Genius in Action

Ally Jewel, a Sex & Intimacy Coach, implemented the AI Genius Marketing Coach in her practice. Here's what she had to say:

"Lisa is a genius! After implementing Lisa's Custom GPT strategy, I created an AI assistant that understands my coaching style perfectly. It helps me generate personalized content for each client, saving me hours every week. The personalized email sequences it helped me create have led to an increase in discovery call bookings. This tool has truly transformed how I market my coaching services."

- Ally Jewel,
Sex & Intimacy Coach

Getting Started with Your AI Genius Marketing Coach

1. **Access the tool:** Visit QR code or here (https://chatgpt.com/g/g-cwmvQzhgl-ai-genius-marketing-coach-content-planner.)
2. **Feed it quality info:** The more you tell it about your business, clients, and goals, the better its outputs will be.
3. **Use it daily:** Make this AI your go-to for all things marketing and content. Regular use helps it learn and adapt to your style.
4. **Experiment and refine:** Try different prompts and approaches. This AI is your playground for innovation.
5. **Combine AI with your expertise:** Use the AI's output as a springboard for your own creativity.

Potential Challenges and How to Overcome Them

1. **Information overload:** Start with one area of your business and gradually expand the AI's use.
2. **Maintaining your voice:** Always review and tweak AI-generated content to ensure it aligns with your brand voice.
3. **Over-reliance:** Remember, the AI is a tool, not a replacement for your expertise. Use it to enhance, not substitute, your coaching skills.

FAQs

Will this AI replace my need for a marketing team? While it can significantly reduce your marketing workload, it's best used in conjunction with human creativity and strategy.

How often should I use this tool? For best results, incorporate it into your daily routine. The more you use it, the better it becomes at understanding your needs.

Is my client data safe with this AI? Always be cautious with client data. Use the AI for general insights and avoid inputting specific client information.

Looking Ahead

As AI continues to evolve, tools like the AI Genius Marketing Coach will become even more sophisticated. They'll offer deeper insights, more personalized recommendations, and even predictive analytics to help you stay ahead of market trends. By embracing this technology now, you're positioning yourself at the forefront of the coaching industry.

Remember, while AI can provide incredible insights and assist in creating elements of your marketing strategy, the essence of your coaching business comes from you. Your unique experiences, philosophy, and approach are what truly make your coaching special. Use this AI tool to amplify your message, reach more people, and free up your time to focus on what you do best – transforming lives.

Action Steps:

1. **Sign up for the AI Genius Marketing Coach** - Content Planner.
2. **Spend an hour inputting information** about your coaching business, ideal clients, and goals.
3. **Use the AI to create a content calendar** for the next month, including blog posts, social media content, and email newsletters.
4. **Generate a detailed client avatar** for your ideal coaching client and use it to refine your marketing messages.
5. **Create an outline** for a new coaching program or service using the AI's suggestions.

By leveraging the power of this custom GPT, you're not just staying current – you're propelling your coaching business into the future. Embrace this tool and watch as your impact grows exponentially.

Key Take Aways:

- AI streamlines the content creation process across various formats
- AI tools help in generating ideas, writing, and optimizing content
- Maintaining your unique voice while leveraging AI is crucial

Action Steps:

1. **Choose three AI tools -** one for writing, one for video, and one for audio. Sign up for free trials.

2. **Use these tools to** create a multi-format content piece: a blog post, a video summary, and an audio version.

3. **Share this content** with your audience and monitor engagement across formats.

4. **Ask for feedback** from trusted clients or colleagues on the AI-assisted content.

5. **Based on results and feedback**, create a plan to incorporate AI into your regular content creation process, focusing on the formats that resonate most with your audience.

Chapter 13
Video Mastery:
High-Impact Marketing with AI

In today's digital landscape, video has become an indispensable tool for coaches looking to connect with their audience on a deeper level. As we've discussed, there's nothing quite like a personal connection, and video is one of the most powerful ways to establish that connection at scale.

Remember, we communicate through five senses: visual, auditory, kinesthetic, olfactory, and gustatory. While we can't engage all five through digital mediums, video allows us to tap into the three most important for coaching: visual, auditory, and to some extent, kinesthetic.

When you use video, you're including more of the senses and engaging people in a way that text alone simply can't match. It allows your audience to see your expressions, hear your tone, and feel your energy. This multi-sensory experience creates a stronger connection and helps build trust more quickly.

Let's look at how AI is revolutionizing video marketing for coaches:

1. AI-designer Video Creation

Tool Spotlight: InVideo

Here you can transform your ideas into professional-looking videos in minutes.

- Turn blog posts into engaging video content
- Create eye-catching promotional videos for your programs
- Develop a series of educational videos for your clients
- Generate scroll-stopping social media video ads

Example: You can use InVideo to turn your "5 Tips for Overcoming Procrastination" blog post into a dynamic video. The AI will suggest relevant stock footage, animations, and text overlays, making your content visually appealing and easy to digest.

Prompt to use: "Create a 90-second video summarizing the key points from my blog post '5 Tips for Overcoming Procrastination'. Use a modern, energetic template suitable for Instagram."

2. Video Editing Made Easy

Tool Spotlight: Descript

- This video editing processes is revolutionary. Edit your video by simply editing the auto-generated transcript
- Remove filler words and awkward pauses automatically
- Create multiple short clips from one long video
- Add captions and transcripts with a single click
- Collaborate with team members in real-time

Example: Imagine recording a 30-minute coaching session. With Descript, you can easily turn this into several short, value-packed videos for social media. The AI will help you identify the most impactful moments and even suggest cuts.

Action Step: Upload your latest long-form video to Descript. Use the AI features to create three short, high-impact clips for social media, each focusing on a key takeaway.

3. Professional-Looking Videos, No Filming Required

Tool Spotlight: Synthesia

This software allows you to create professional videos using AI avatars.

- Create customized welcome videos for each new client
- Develop a video FAQ section for your website
- Produce multilingual versions of your content
- Create video course materials without stepping in front of a camera

Example: You could use Synthesia to create personalized welcome videos for your group coaching program. Each video could address the client by name and mention their specific goals, all using an AI avatar that looks and sounds just like you.

Prompt to use: "Create a 60-second welcome video for my new client [Name]. Mention their goal of [specific goal] and how our 12-week coaching program will help them achieve it. Use a friendly, professional tone."

4. Live Streaming with AI Assistance

Tool Spotlight: Restream

While not entirely AI-equipped, Restream has AI features that can elevate your live streaming:

- Stream to multiple platforms simultaneously
- Use AI-operated chat translation for global audience engagement
- Leverage smart scheduling for optimal viewing times
- Analyze performance with AI-enhanced analytics

Example: You could use Restream to host a live Q&A session, streaming simultaneously to YouTube, Facebook, and LinkedIn. The AI chat translation feature would allow you to engage with a global audience in real-time.

Action Step: Plan a live streaming event using Restream. Use the AI scheduling feature to determine the best time for your audience and prepare to engage with viewers in multiple languages.

5. Video Personalization at Scale

Tool Spotlight: Tavus

This AI tool allows you to create personalized videos at scale:

- Send personalized video messages to hundreds of leads
- Create custom video experiences for each stage of your sales funnel
- Develop personalized video follow-ups after discovery calls

Example: Imagine sending a personalized video to each person who signs up for your free webinar. The video could mention their name and reference the specific pain point they indicated when signing up. This level of personalization can significantly boost engagement and conversion rates.

Prompt to use: "Create a template for a 30-second personalized video thanking [Name] for signing up for my webinar on [Topic]. Mention that we'll address their specific challenge of [Challenge] during the session."

6. AI-Enhanced Video Analytics

Tool Spotlight: Clarity.Video

Clarity, developed by my friend and associate Todd Hartley, video authority and expert, offers powerful AI-driven analytics tailored for business entrepreneurs and coaches:

- Track viewer engagement with detailed heat maps
- Use AI to identify your most effective video content
- Get AI-generated suggestions for video optimization
- Understand your audience better with demographic insights

Example: With Clarity.video, you might discover that viewers consistently rewatch the section where you explain a particular coaching technique. This insight could lead you to create more content around this popular topic, directly addressing your audience's interests.

You might also find that different audience segments prefer different video styles. Perhaps younger viewers engage more with shorter, dynamic videos, while older viewers prefer in-depth content. This allows you to tailor your video strategy for maximum impact.

Action Step: Upload your three most recent coaching videos to Clarity.video. After a week, analyze the AI-generated insights to identify:

- The most engaging parts of each video
- Patterns in viewer behavior
- Demographic information about your most engaged viewers

Use these insights to plan your next set of videos, focusing on content and styles that resonate most with your audience. By leveraging Clarity.video's AI-enabled analytics, you can create a data-driven video strategy that boosts engagement and grows your coaching business.

7. AI-Generated Video Repurposing

Tool Spotlight: Vidyo.ai

Vidyo.ai is a video editing and repurposing platform that can help you maximize the impact of your long-form video content.

- Turn long videos into short, engaging clips optimized for social media
- Automatically identify key moments in your videos
- Create multiple versions of your content tailored for different platforms
- Add captions and text overlays to increase engagement

Example: Let's say you've recorded an hour-long webinar on "10 Strategies for Business Growth." You can feed this video into Vidyo.ai, and it will automatically create several short, engaging clips, each focusing on one strategy. These clips can be easily shared on platforms like Instagram, TikTok, or LinkedIn, dramatically increasing your content's reach and engagement.

Action Step: Take your latest long-form video content (like a webinar or lengthy YouTube video) and use Vidyo.ai to create a series of 60-second clips for Instagram and TikTok. Monitor the engagement on these shorter clips compared to your usual content.

By incorporating Vidyo.ai into your video marketing strategy, you can significantly increase the mileage you get out of each piece of video content, ensuring your message reaches a wider audience across multiple platforms.

Case Study: AI-Powered Video Marketing Success

Let me share a success story that illustrates the power of AI in video marketing. Coach Katie was overworked with trying to create consistent, engaging video content for her leadership coaching business. She decided to implement AI-powered video tools and employ her virtual assistant to help. Here's what happened:

- Using InVideo, she turned her top 10 blog posts into visually appealing videos, doubling her content output

- With Descript, she edited past videos effortlessly, cutting her editing time by 75%

- Synthesia allowed her to create personalized welcome videos for each new client, increasing her onboarding engagement

- Using Restream, she hosted a live Q&A session that reached audiences across three platforms simultaneously, tripling her usual live viewership

- Tavus enabled her to send personalized video follow-ups to webinar attendees, boosting her conversion rate from 5% to 15%

- Clarity.Video's insights helped her optimize her content strategy, leading to a 40% increase in overall video engagement

The result? Katie's engagements with clients increased. All while spending less time on video creation and more time coaching.

Katie says, "AI has transformed every aspect of my business including my video marketing. I'm creating more content, reaching more people, and seeing better results than ever before. It's like having a full video production team at my fingertips."

Remember, the goal of using AI in your video marketing isn't to remove your personality from the equation. Rather, it's to amplify your message, reach more people, and free up your time to focus on what you do best.

Key Takeaways:

- AI enhances video creation, editing, and distribution
- AI tools can create personalized video content at scale
- Video analytics powered by AI provide deeper insights into audience engagement

Action Steps:

1. Choose one AI video creation tool and one editing tool from this chapter. Sign up for free trials.
2. Create a short (1-2 minute) video introducing yourself and your coaching services using the AI video creation tool.
3. Use the AI video editing tool to create three 30-second clips from this video, each highlighting a different aspect of your services.
4. Share these videos on your social media platforms and monitor engagement.
5. Measure performance of these videos and create a plan for incorporating regular AI-assisted video content into your marketing strategy.

With these AI video tools at your disposal; you're now equipped to create high-impact video marketing that resonates with your audience and grows your coaching business. Lights, camera, AI, action!

Chapter 14
Writing Your Book with AI
- The Power of Your Voice

*I*n the world of coaching, authoring a book can be a game-changer. It establishes your authority, attracts clients, and opens doors to speaking engagements. But the process of writing a book can be daunting. This is where AI comes in, not to replace your voice, but to amplify it and streamline the writing process.

My journey with book writing has been a fascinating evolution, perfectly mirroring the advancements in technology and AI. Let me take you through this journey:

My first book, "Fine to Fab," was a labor of love, written entirely from the heart. It delved deep into understanding why we sabotage ourselves and how smart people can sometimes do stupid things. The book was all about transforming from feeling F.I.N.E. (F'd up, Insecure, Neurotic, and Emotional) to truly being FAB (Fabulous, Awesome, Beautiful).

For my second book, "Brand You, Become the Expert," I collaborated with an associate. We focused on a step-by-step guide to building your Personal Unique Brand ™ for more sales, more clients, more often.

Then came my third book, "How to Build a Seven-Figure Coaching Business: Bonus Using AI" This was my first foray into using AI in the writing process. I was just dipping my toes into the AI waters at this point, but I could already see the potential.

Now, using AI to write books is a completely different ball game. I remember paying thousands of dollars to a famous New York Times bestselling author to teach me how to write books. While that was valuable, I soon discovered there were easier, more efficient ways to create impactful books.

But let me be clear: your book is more than just words on a page. **It's your hook, your credibility, your authority**. It's a powerful door opener. And with AI, you can write a book in a weekend if you want to. But if you're aiming for something really good, it might take a bit longer – maybe a weekend plus a couple of weeks to gather all the resources you need to write an amazing book.

> **The secret? Speak your book.** That's exactly what I'm doing with this book you're holding right now. I'm speaking it, then taking the transcriptions and feeding them into AI. The AI helps break it down into chapters and sub-chapters, refine it, and transform it into something usable and amazing.

> **Why is this approach so important?** Because it ensures that the book is truly yours. It's your story, your voice, not just something an AI churned out. You have a book in you, and this process is about giving your information to the world. AI is simply a catalyst to make it even better than it already was, to give you the structure and knowledge you might not have had, to help you formulate it properly, write it eloquently, and interweave your stories with class and ease.

The most powerful books come from your unique experiences, insights, and voice. AI is not here to replace you as an author, but to amplify your message and streamline the writing process.

Now, let me walk you through the step-by-step process of how you can use this method to write your own powerful, authentic book with the assistance of AI:

Here's how to create a book that's genuinely yours, with AI as your assistant:

> **Identify Your Avatar and Their Needs:** Use AI to help you deep dive into your ideal reader's profile. Prompt: "Help me create a detailed avatar for the ideal reader of my book on [your topic]. Include their pain points, desires, and what they're looking for in a 'how-to' book."

> **Craft Your Book Concept** with your avatar in mind, use AI to brainstorm book ideas. Prompt: "Based on this avatar [paste avatar description], generate 10 book concepts that would solve their most pressing problems related to [your area of expertise]."

> **Create Your Book Outline Use AI** to help structure your book. Prompt: "Create a detailed chapter-by-chapter outline for a book titled [your chosen title]. Include main points to cover in each chapter."

> **Generate Interview Questions:** Have AI create questions that will help you delve even deeper into each chapter's content. Prompt: "Based on this chapter outline [paste outline], generate 20 in-depth questions that will help me explore all aspects of this topic, including opportunities for me to share personal stories and experiences."

Speak Your Book Set up a Zoom call (you can do this solo) and record yourself answering these questions, sharing stories, and exploring each chapter's content. Speak naturally, as if you're explaining these concepts to a client or friend.

Transcribe Your Recording: Use a transcription service or AI tool to convert your spoken words into text. I like to attach the APP, Fathom to zoom as it will record the transcript and is easy to search out things you are looking for within it. Otter is another great option.

Refine with AI Feed your transcript into ChatGPT or Claude. Prompt: "This is a transcript of me speaking about [topic]. Please organize this content into coherent chapters based on the outline [paste outline]. Maintain my speaking style and voice but improve flow and readability where necessary. Ensure all my stories and personal insights are preserved."

Review and Personalize: Go through the AI-organized content. This is your chance to add more personal touches, clarify points, and ensure the book truly reflects your voice and expertise.

Polish and Format: Use AI to help with final edits and formatting. Prompt: "Please format this book content with proper chapter headings, subheadings, and ensure consistent styling throughout. Flag any areas that might need further clarification or expansion."

Create Supporting Elements: Use AI to help generate ideas for your book's title, subtitle, back cover blurb, and marketing materials. Always review and personalize these elements to ensure they align with your voice and message.

Remember, the key is that YOU are the author. AI is simply a tool to help organize your thoughts, streamline the process, and enhance your natural writing style. The stories, insights, and expertise are all yours.

By following this method, you're creating a book that truly captures your voice and expertise. Your readers will connect with your authentic experiences and insights, making the book a powerful tool for attracting ideal clients and establishing your authority in your niche.

This book you're holding is a testament to this process. It's my voice, my experiences, and my expertise, organized and enhanced with the help of AI. It's a blend of human insight and technological efficiency, creating a resource that I hope will truly serve you in building your coaching business.

Overcoming Common Challenges

Writer's Block: Use AI to generate prompts or ideas when you're stuck. But always infuse these with your own experiences and insights.

Maintaining Consistency: AI can help ensure your tone and style remain consistent throughout the book. Use it to flag any inconsistencies.

Time Management: Set realistic goals. Even with AI assistance, quality writing takes time. Use AI to help create a writing schedule and stick to it.

Balancing AI and Authenticity: Always review AI-generated content critically. Your unique voice and experiences are what make your book valuable.

Key Take Aways:

- AI can assist in every stage of the book writing process
- Speaking your book and using AI for refinement maintains your authentic voice
- AI helps in structuring, editing, and even marketing your book

Action Steps:

1. **Define your book's avatar** and core concept using the AI prompts provided.

2. Create your detailed outline with AI assistance.

3. Generate a list of in-depth questions for each chapter.

4. **Schedule** a day to "speak" your book, recording your responses and stories.

5. **Get your recording transcribed** and use AI to help organize it into a coherent manuscript.

6. **Review, refine,** and add personal touches to ensure the book truly reflects your voice.

Remember, your unique insights and experiences are what make your book valuable. Use AI as a tool to amplify your voice, not replace it. Happy writing!

Chapter 15
AI Tools Reference Guide

This comprehensive guide provides an overview of all the AI tools mentioned in the book. Each tool is described with its key features and potential applications in your coaching business. Use this chapter as a quick reference when implementing AI strategies in your practice.

As the AI landscape evolves rapidly, this guide aims to provide you with a solid foundation of tools to start with. Remember, while these tools are powerful, the key to success lies in how you apply them to your unique coaching practice. Always experiment, adapt, and find the combination that works best for you.

ChatGPT / GPT-4o / Soon GPT-5

A powerful language model for generating human-like text. Use for content creation, brainstorming, generating ideas, and answering complex questions.

Example Prompt: "Generate 10 blog post ideas for female entrepreneurs looking to scale their businesses."

Claude AI

An AI assistant capable of engaging in human-like conversations and completing various tasks. Like ChatGPT, use for content creation, analysis, and problem-solving.

Example Prompt: "Create an outline for a blog post on '5 Ways to Overcome Self-Doubt as an Entrepreneur.'

Gemini by Anthropic

An AI model focused on open-ended conversation and task completion. Engage in freeform dialogue, get help with analysis and writing tasks, and receive thoughtful responses. Gemini aims to be helpful, harmless, and honest.

Example Prompt: "I'm developing a new group coaching program for entrepreneurs. Can you help me brainstorm a list of potential topics to cover in the program, focusing on the key challenges faced by small business owners?"

Jasper AI

AI-driven writing assistant for creating marketing copy and content. Generate blog posts, social media content, and marketing materials.

Example Prompt: "Write an engaging Instagram caption for a post about overcoming self-doubt, including relevant hashtags."

Copy.ai

AI tool for creating marketing copy and content. Generate social media posts, ad copy, and product descriptions.

Example Prompt: "Create a series of LinkedIn posts discussing the benefits of personalized coaching."

Surfer SEO

AI-generated SEO optimization tool. Optimize your content for search engines and improve rankings.

Example Prompt: "Analyze my blog post on 'Top Marketing Strategies for Female Entrepreneurs' and provide SEO recommendations."

InVideo

AI-operated video creation tool. Create professional videos from text, images, automated text-to-speech and voice-over capabilities and other video clips.

Example Usage: Create an engaging promotional video for your upcoming group coaching program. Select a template that aligns with your brand, customize the text and images, and add a compelling voice-over using InVideo's AI-powered text-to-speech feature.

Descript

AI-enhanced video and audio editing software. Edit videos by editing text, remove filler words, and create transcripts.

Example Prompt: "Edit my 5-minute video to remove filler words and add captions."

VEED

Online video editing platform with AI features. Add subtitles, remove background noise, and create animated text overlays.

Example Prompt: "Create animated text overlays for my promotional video."

Eleven Labs

AI voice generation platform. Create realistic AI voices for voiceovers and audio content.

Example Prompt: "Generate a professional voiceover for my coaching introduction video."

Resemble.AI

Advanced AI voice cloning and synthesis platform. Create realistic AI voices for personalized messaging and voice-overs in multiple languages.

Example Prompt: "Clone my voice and generate a welcome message for new coaching clients in both English and Spanish."

FakeYou

Text-to-speech platform with a vast library of voices. Generate speech from text using a wide variety of **pre-existing and custom voices**.

Example Prompt: "Convert this script about time management techniques into speech using a motivational speaker-style voice."

SalesStack.ai

AI-powered sales enablement platform to optimize the entire sales process. Automate lead generation, email outreach, meeting scheduling, and follow-ups for coaching services. Higher pricing compared to some others.

Example Prompt: "Generate a list of 50 potential leads for my executive coaching program, with personalized outreach messages for each."

HeyGen

AI-generated video creation platform. Create videos with AI presenters and translate content into multiple languages.

Example Prompt: "Create a video with an AI presenter introducing my new coaching program."

Synthesia

AI video creation platform using virtual avatars. Create professional-looking videos without filming, including multilingual versions.

Example Prompt: "Generate a multilingual version of my coaching welcome video."

MobileMonkey

AI-operated chatbot platform. Create chatbots for customer service and lead generation.

Example Prompt: "Set up a chatbot for my website to handle customer inquiries."

ManyChat

Another AI-drivenn chatbot platform. Build chatbots for Facebook Messenger and other platforms.

Example Prompt: "Create a Facebook Messenger bot to automate responses to common questions."

Headlime

Description: AI-fueled copywriting tool. Generate landing page copy and headlines. Example Prompt: "Write a compelling headline for my coaching services landing page."

Reply.io

AI-enhanced email outreach and sales engagement platform. Automate and personalize email campaigns.

Example Prompt: "Generate a series of personalized email templates for my lead nurturing campaign."

Albert.ai

AI-driven digital marketing platform. Optimize digital ad campaigns across multiple channels.

Example Prompt: "Optimize my Facebook ad campaign to increase conversions."

Zapier

While not strictly an AI tool, it can be used to automate workflows with AI-like functionality. Create automated workflows between different apps and services.

Example Prompt: "Set up a workflow to automatically post new blog articles to my social media accounts."

Content at Scale

AI content creation platform. Generate long-form content and blog posts at scale.

Example Prompt: "Write a 1500-word blog post on 'Building a Strong Online Presence for Your Business.'"

Canva (with Magic Write)

Graphic design platform with AI-generated writing assistant. Create visuals and write accompanying text for social media and marketing materials.

Example Prompt: "Design an Instagram post with a quote on entrepreneurship and generate a caption."

Restream

Live streaming platform with AI features. Stream to multiple platforms simultaneously and engage with a global audience.

Example Prompt: "Set up a live stream for my upcoming webinar on multiple social media platforms."

Tavus

AI video personalization platform. Create personalized video messages at scale.

Example Prompt: "Generate personalized thank-you video messages for my new clients."

Clarity.video

AI-driven video analytics platform. Analyze viewer engagement and optimize video content.

Example Usage: Analyze my latest video for viewer engagement and suggest improvements.

Vidyo.ai

AI-generated video editing and repurposing platform. Turn long videos into short, engaging clips optimized for social media.

Example Prompt: "Create a series of 1-minute clips from my latest webinar for Instagram and TikTok."

Grammarly

AI writing assistant that helps with grammar, spelling, and style improvements. Improve the quality of your writing in emails, blog posts, social media content, and more.

Example Prompt: "Check this blog post for grammatical errors and suggest style improvements."

Lately.ai

AI-driven content creation and social media marketing platform. Repurpose long-form content into social media posts and optimize content distribution.

Example Prompt: "Convert this webinar transcript into a series of engaging social media posts."

BuzzSumo

AI content research and social media analytics tool. Discover trending topics, analyze competitors, and find key influencers.

Example Prompt: "Find the most shared articles on 'coaching business growth' in the last month."

HubSpot

AI-enhanced CRM platform with marketing, sales, and service tools. Manage customer relationships, automate marketing tasks, and track campaign performance.

Example Prompt: "Set up an automated email marketing campaign for new coaching clients."

Piktochart

AI-generated infographics and visual content creation tool. Create visually appealing infographics, presentations, and reports.

Example Prompt: "Design an infographic summarizing the benefits of personalized coaching."

CoSchedule Headline Analyzer

AI tool for analyzing and improving headlines. Craft compelling headlines that boost engagement and click-through rates.

Example Prompt: "Analyze this headline: '10 Proven Strategies to Scale Your Coaching Business.'"

Crimson Hexagon (now Brandwatch)

AI-generated social media listening and analytics platform. Monitor brand mentions, analyze sentiment, and track social media trends.

Example Prompt: "Analyze social media sentiment around the term 'business coaching.'"

A-Weber/Mail Chimp

AI-enhanced email marketing platform. Create, send, and analyze email campaigns with automation features.

Example Prompt: "Generate a series of welcome emails for new newsletter subscribers."

ActiveCampaign

AI marketing automation platform. Automate email marketing, customer segmentation, and sales follow-ups.

Example Prompt: "Create an automated workflow for nurturing leads into coaching clients."

Awario

AI-driven social media monitoring and analytics tool. Track brand mentions, analyze sentiment, and identify industry influencers.

Example Prompt: "Monitor social media for mentions of 'online coaching' and provide sentiment analysis."

Otter.ai

AI-driven transcription and note-taking tool. Transcribe audio and video recordings, generate meeting notes, and create searchable archives of conversations.

Example Prompt: "Transcribe my coaching session recording and highlight key action items."

Fathom

AI-generated meeting assistant and note-taking tool. Automatically take notes during video calls, generate summaries, and create action items.

Example Prompt: "Summarize my client strategy call and extract the main discussion points and action items."

Midjourney

AI-designed image generation tool. Create unique, high-quality images based on text descriptions.

Example Prompt: "Generate a professional, modern logo for a life coaching business focused on career transitions."

DALL-E

AI image generation model by OpenAI. Create original, realistic images and art from text descriptions.

Example Prompt: "Create an inspiring image representing personal growth and success for my coaching website header."

Ideogram

AI-fueled design and image creation tool. Generate custom graphics, logos, and visual content based on text prompts. Good for social media, book covers, memes.

Example Prompt: "Design a set of icons representing different aspects of life coaching: career, relationships, health, and finance."

Google Trends

While not strictly AI, it uses machine learning to analyze search trends. Research trending topics, compare interest over time, and identify seasonal patterns in your niche.

Example Prompt: "Compare the search interest for 'life coaching' and 'business coaching' over the past year."

Answer The Public

Uses machine learning to generate questions people are asking about topics. Discover content ideas, understand audience questions, and inform your content strategy.

Example Prompt: "Show me the most common questions people ask about 'starting a coaching business.'"

Ubersuggest

AI-driven SEO and content marketing tool. Conduct keyword research, analyze competitors, and generate content ideas.

Example Prompt: "Find long-tail keywords related to 'executive coaching' with low competition and high search volume."

As the AI landscape continues to evolve, keep an eye on these emerging tools that show promise for coaches:

1. **GPT-4 and beyond:** Future iterations of large language models that may offer even more advanced capabilities.
2. **AI-powered virtual reality coaching platforms:** For immersive coaching experiences.
3. **Emotion AI tools:** To help coaches better understand and respond to clients' emotional states.
4. **Predictive analytics platforms:** To forecast client outcomes and tailor coaching strategies.

Remember to stay updated on the latest AI developments and always evaluate new tools based on their potential to enhance your unique coaching practice.

Key Take Aways:

- There's a wide range of AI tools available for various aspects of your coaching business
- Experiment with different tools to find the ones that best suit your needs
- Always use AI tools ethically and in compliance with data protection regulations

Action Steps:

1. **Choose three AI tools** from this list that align with your immediate business needs.

2. **Sign up for free trials** or explore free versions of these tools.

3. **Implement one AI tool** in your workflow this week and document the results.

4. **Set a quarterly reminder** to review and update your AI toolkit based on new developments and your evolving business needs.

Chapter 16
Future Horizons: Emerging AI Trends in Coaching

Hey there, future-focused coach! Can you feel the excitement? We're on the cusp of some mind-blowing developments in AI that are going to revolutionize the way we coach. Let's peek into the crystal ball and explore what's coming our way.

1. Hyper-Personalization: Your AI Wingman

Imagine having an AI sidekick that knows your client better than they know themselves. Crazy, right? But that's where we're headed. This AI will be like a super-smart assistant, analyzing everything from your client's sleep patterns to their work productivity. It'll help you tailor your coaching so precisely; it'll feel like mind-reading.

I can already hear some of you saying, "But Lisa, isn't that a bit... creepy?" I get it. We'll need to be extra careful about privacy and data security. But think about the possibilities! You'll be able to offer insights and support that are so spot-on, your clients will wonder if you've got psychic powers.

2. Virtual Reality Coaching: Welcome to the Matrix

Okay, not quite the Matrix, but close! Virtual and Augmented Reality are going to take experiential learning to a whole new level. Picture this: you're working with a client on public speaking. Instead of just talking about it, you can transport them to a virtual TED stage, complete with a responsive audience. How cool is that?

Of course, we'll need to make sure everyone can use this tech easily. We don't want to leave anyone behind in our real world while we're playing in virtual ones!

3. Emotion AI: The Digital Empath

We're about to get an AI that can read emotions better than some humans! It'll analyze facial expressions, tone of voice, even word choice, giving you real-time insights into your client's emotional state. Note: This is already happening on many platforms. I've been getting emotional scores on my zoom meetings for years now.

Now, don't worry – this isn't about replacing your emotional intelligence. Think of it more like an emotional hearing aid, amplifying your natural empathy. You'll still be the heart and soul of the coaching relationship.

4. AI: Your Personal Professional Development Guru

Imagine having a mentor who never sleeps, is always up to date with the latest in coaching and knows exactly what you need to learn next. That's what AI-driven continuous learning will be like. It'll analyze your coaching sessions, keep an eye on industry trends, and serve up personalized learning opportunities.

The challenge? Making sure you're still steering your own development. After all, you know yourself best!

5. Predictive Analytics: Your Coaching Crystal Ball

We're not quite at the point of predicting lottery numbers, but AI will soon be able to forecast coaching outcomes with impressive accuracy. By analyzing data from thousands of coaching engagements, it'll help you set realistic goals and anticipate potential roadblocks.

Remember though, we're not fortune tellers. This is about being prepared, not predetermined. Your intuition and flexibility will still be key!

6. Wearables and IoT: Coaching in Real-Time

Wearable tech is about to give us superpowers. Imagine getting real-time data on your client's stress levels, sleep quality, or even posture. For those of us in wellness or performance coaching, this is going to be a game-changer.

Of course, with great power comes great responsibility. We'll need to be mindful of information overload and always prioritize our clients' privacy.

7. Natural Language Processing: The AI Translator

Soon, AI will understand nuance and context so well, it'll be like having a universal translator for coach-speak. It'll help you communicate more effectively, especially when managing multiple clients.

But don't worry, it won't replace your voice. Think of it more as an amplifier, helping your unique coaching style reach more people more effectively.

8. Ethical AI: Keeping It Real and Right

As AI becomes more integrated into our coaching practices, we'll need to up our game in terms of ethics and transparency. We might see industry-standard AI ethics certifications popping up.

This isn't just about following rules – it's about maintaining the trust that's at the heart of every coaching relationship. We'll need to be open with our clients about how we're using AI and how their data is protected.

The Future is Bright (and AI-Powered)!

Exciting times ahead, right? But remember, all these fancy AI tools are just that – tools. They're here to enhance your coaching, not replace you. You're still the secret sauce in the coaching relationship.

So, what's your next move? Here are a few ideas:

1. Pick one of these trends that really speaks to you. How could you start incorporating it into your practice?

2. Set up some Google Alerts for AI in coaching. Stay in the know!

3. Block out some time every few months to review and update your AI strategy.

4. Join some online communities focused on AI in coaching. There's nothing like learning from fellow pioneers!

5. Consider teaming up with some tech-savvy folks to explore how these trends could work in your specific coaching niche.

Remember, the future of coaching isn't about AI replacing the human touch. It's about AI helping us touch more lives, more effectively. So, are you ready to ride this AI wave to new heights in your coaching practice? Let's do this!

Chapter 17
Your Journey to AI Mastery - Next Steps

*C*ongratulations! You've just completed an exhilarating journey into the world of AI-powered coaching. Let's take a moment to reflect on what you've learned and chart your course forward.

Throughout this book, we've explored how AI can revolutionize every aspect of your coaching practice:

1. **Mindset and Growth:** We discussed the importance of adopting a growth mindset when it comes to AI, seeing it as a powerful ally rather than a threat.

2. **Client Avatars and Niching:** You learned how to use AI to create detailed client avatars and find your perfect niche, allowing you to target your ideal clients with precision.

3. **High-Ticket Programs:** We explored how AI can help you design, price, and sell premium coaching offers that provide immense value to your clients.

4. Branding and Marketing: You discovered how AI can assist in crafting a unique brand identity and creating marketing strategies that resonate with your audience.

5. **Sales Funnels:** We delved into how AI can optimize your sales funnels, from lead generation to conversion.

6. **Client Communication:** You learned about AI tools that can automate and personalize your client interactions, enhancing engagement and retention.

7. **Content Creation:** We explored a variety of AI tools for creating blog posts, social media content, and engaging videos.

8. **Video Marketing:** You discovered how AI can help you create, edit, and analyze video content for maximum impact.

Where to Start

Now, you might be wondering, "This is all great, but where do I begin?" Here's a roadmap to help you implement what you've learned:

1. **Assess Your Current State:** Before diving in, take stock of your current business processes. Identify areas where you're spending the most time or facing the biggest challenges. These are prime candidates for AI integration.

2. **Start Small:** Choose one area of your business to focus on first. Perhaps begin with content creation or email marketing automation. Success in one area will build your confidence to expand to others.

3. **Experiment:** Sign up for free trials of the AI tools mentioned here. Spend time exploring their features and understanding how they can fit into your workflow. Don't be afraid to try multiple tools to find the best fit.

4. **Measure Results:** As you implement AI tools, track your results meticulously. Are you saving time? Seeing better engagement? Increasing conversions? Use these metrics to guide your AI strategy and justify further investments.

5. **Upskill:** Dedicate time each week to learning more about AI. The field is rapidly evolving, and staying informed will help you leverage new opportunities as they arise. Consider joining online courses or attending webinars specific to AI in coaching.

6. **Build a Support Network:** Connect with other coaches who are also implementing AI. Share experiences, troubleshoot challenges, and celebrate successes together.

Getting the Most Out of This Book

To truly maximize the value of this book:

1. **Review the Action Steps:** At the end of each chapter. Make a plan to implement these over the next few months. Create a timeline and hold yourself accountable.

2. **Use the AI Tools Reference Guide:** Refer back to the comprehensive list of AI tools provided. Experiment with different tools to find what works best for you. Keep notes on your experiences with each tool.

3. **Leverage the Custom GPT:** I've done the heavy lifting for you and created a custom GPT specifically for you, called **"AI Genius Marketing Coach - Content Planner"**. You can access it at QR Code here. This tool can help you create content calendars, generate social media posts, and even draft blog articles. Make it a part of your regular workflow.

4. **Join the AI for Coaches Community:** Connect with other coaches who are on the same journey. Share experiences, ask questions, and learn from each other. The collective wisdom of this others can be invaluable. Join us here now!

5. **Revisit Regularly:** As you implement AI in your business, come back to relevant chapters. You'll likely find new insights as you gain more experience with AI.

Remember, the goal of implementing AI in your coaching business is not to remove the human element, but to enhance it. AI should free you up to do more of what you do best – connecting with clients, providing insights, and transforming lives.

To help you get started, here's a 90-day implementation roadmap:

Days 1-30: Foundation

- Choose one AI tool for content creation (e.g., ChatGPT or Jasper)
- Create a content calendar for the next month using AI assistance
- Implement an AI-powered chatbot on your website

Days 31-60: Expansion

- Integrate an AI tool for email marketing automation
- Create your first AI-assisted video using tools like InVideo or Synthesia
- Use AI to optimize your website for SEO

Days 61-90: Optimization

- Analyze the results of your AI implementations so far
- Refine your AI-generated marketing funnel
- Explore advanced AI applications like personalized client experiences or predictive analytics

Remember, this is a suggested timeline. Feel free to adjust based on your specific needs and pace.

Your Next Steps

1. **Review the action steps** at the end of each chapter. Choose three that resonate most with you and implement them in the next 30 days. Set specific goals and deadlines for each.

2. **Experiment with the custom GPT** I've created for you. Use it to plan your content strategy for the next month. Pay attention to how it changes your content creation process.

3. **Schedule a "Strategy Day"** with yourself or your team to map out how AI will fit into your business operations over the next 6-12 months. Create a phased implementation plan.

4. **Start an "AI Learning Journal"** where you document your experiences, insights, and results as you implement these tools. This will be invaluable as you refine your approach.

5. **Identify one repetitive task** in your business that takes up a lot of your time. Research AI tools that could help automate this task and implement a solution within the next two weeks.

A Personal Invitation

If you're feeling excited about the possibilities but also a bit overwhelmed, know that you're not alone. Implementing AI in your coaching business is a journey, and sometimes it helps to have a guide.

That's why I want to extend a personal invitation. If you'd like to see what it looks like to work with me and get personalized guidance on implementing AI in your coaching business, I encourage you to apply for a strategy session at www.callwithlisa.com.

In this session, we'll discuss your specific business challenges and determine what a personalized AI strategy for implementation tailored to your specific needs and goals would look like. We will discuss multiple methods for incorporating AI into all aspects of your coaching practice.

The future of coaching is here, and it's AI-enhanced. By embracing these tools, you're not just future-proofing your business – you're setting yourself up to make an even bigger impact, reach more clients, and achieve the success you've always dreamed of.

Remember, this book is not the end of your AI journey – it's just the beginning. Keep exploring, keep learning, and keep pushing the boundaries of what's possible in your coaching business.

Here's to your AI-powered success!

Bonus:
Supercharge Your Coaching Business with AI Power Prompts

Wow…future AI-powered coaching superstar! Can you feel the excitement? We're about to turbocharge your business with some seriously powerful AI prompts.

Now, I know what you're thinking. "Lisa, I've learned so much already, my brain is about to explode!" Don't worry, I've got you covered. This bonus chapter is like your personal AI cheat sheet. It's packed with ready-to-use prompts that'll have you leveraging AI like a pro in no time.

Remember when we talked about working smarter, not harder? Well, these prompts are your shortcut to doing just that. We're covering everything from plotting your business strategy to crafting killer marketing campaigns and keeping your clients coming back for more.

Think of these prompts as your secret weapon. They're designed to help you squeeze every ounce of value out of tools like ChatGPT. Once you start using these, you'll wonder how you ever managed without them.

Now, here's the deal: these prompts are awesome, but they're not set in stone. Feel free to tweak them, mix them up, and make them your own. After all, your unique coaching magic is what sets you apart.

So, are you ready to supercharge your coaching business? Then get going and show the world what an AI-powered coach can really do!

But, before we do, let's hear from one of my clients who has experienced the transformative power of AI-driven coaching strategies firsthand:

Real-World Success: The Power of AI in Action

"Lisa's expertise in AI-driven marketing is nothing short of awe inspiring. Her expertise on AI is a game-changer that will leave readers absolutely Wowed-it's Awesome!

Working with Lisa to build out my marketing plan was an extraordinary experience. From crafting my signature talk to developing a comprehensive 6-week program, Lisa's guidance was invaluable.

She even helped me record content to leverage AI for marketing, covering everything from Zoom sessions to social media, text campaigns, JV partnerships, content creation, program development, lead magnets, and precise pricing strategies.

What struck me most was the incredible efficiency. We accomplished in just 4 days what had previously taken 6 months. This wasn't my first rodeo with Lisa - a few years back, her coaching helped me generate over $142k in just a few months when I was getting my practice off the ground.

She truly is an expert who knows exactly what to do. Returning to work with Lisa on my new program and talk was a no-brainer.

Her mastery of AI, combined with her proven '7 Figure Talk That Sells' and 'Mastery to Millions' strategies, elevated our work to unprecedented levels of excellence.

The experience was beyond stellar - it was magnificent, unbelievable, and surpassed my wildest dreams and expectations. The speed and intelligence with which we implemented AI, guided by Lisa's decades of marketing and sales experience, accelerated our progress far beyond what I could have achieved alone.

Words like 'above and beyond,' 'stellar,' and 'magnificent' only begin to describe the transformative impact of working with Lisa. If you're looking to revolutionize your business and marketing strategies with AI, Lisa is the expert you need.

Her book and coaching will undoubtedly propel you to new heights of success. It's an investment that will pay dividends for years to come. Run...Don't Walk. You won't regret it!"

- Ally Jewel,
Sex & Intimacy Coach

Ally's experience showcases the incredible potential of combining AI with strategic coaching. Now, let's explore how you can harness this power in your own coaching business with these AI-powered prompts.

Business Strategy and Planning

Vision and Goals: "As a coach serving [your niche], create a compelling 12-month vision for my business. Include three measurable goals that will propel me towards seven figures, considering my current revenue of [your current revenue]. Factor in market trends like [trend 1] and [trend 2]."

SWOT Analysis: "Conduct a detailed SWOT analysis for my coaching business, focusing on [your specific coaching area]. For each category, provide 3-5 points. Then, suggest three actionable strategies to leverage my strengths and opportunities while mitigating weaknesses and threats."

Revenue Streams: "Based on my expertise in [your area of expertise] and my target audience of [your ideal client], generate five innovative revenue stream ideas. For each idea, provide a brief description, potential pricing strategy, and estimated time investment. Rank these ideas based on their potential ROI and alignment with my brand."

Marketing and Branding

Brand Positioning: "Craft a powerful brand positioning statement for my coaching business that sets me apart from competitors like [competitor 1] and [competitor 2]. Incorporate my unique approach of [your unique method or philosophy] and how it specifically benefits [your ideal client]."

Marketing Plan: "Design a comprehensive 90-day marketing plan for my coaching business. Include a mix of content marketing, social media, email campaigns, and one innovative marketing tactic. Provide week-by-week action items, focusing on attracting [your ideal client] and promoting [your signature program]."

SEO Optimization: "Develop an SEO strategy to boost my coaching website's ranking. Identify 10 high-value, low-competition keywords related to [your coaching niche]. Then, outline a content plan that incorporates these keywords, including blog post ideas, meta descriptions, and internal linking strategies."

Content Creation

Content Strategy: "Create a dynamic content strategy that positions me as the go-to expert in [your coaching niche]. Include a 3-month content calendar with themes, topics, and content types (blog, video, podcast, social media).

Ensure each piece addresses a specific pain point of [your ideal client] and aligns with my signature program, [your program name]."

Engaging Blog Posts: "Generate 10 attention-grabbing blog post titles that speak directly to the challenges faced by [your ideal client]. Then, for the most compelling title, create a detailed outline for a 2000-word ultimate guide, including subheadings, key points, and a powerful call-to-action promoting [your coaching service]."

Video Marketing: "Develop a script for a 2-minute YouTube video that introduces my signature coaching program, [program name]. Include a hook, three key benefits, a client success story, and a clear call-to-action. Also, provide ideas for 5 shorter videos (30-60 seconds each) that can be repurposed for Instagram Reels and TikTok."

Client Engagement and Retention

Onboarding Experience: "Design a premium onboarding experience for new clients in my [program name] coaching program. Include a welcome email series, a personalized video message script, and ideas for a physical welcome package. Focus on making clients feel valued and setting the stage for transformational results."

Retention Strategy: "Create a 6-month client retention strategy that keeps clients engaged and achieving results. Include ideas for check-in sessions, progress tracking tools, exclusive resources, and a loyalty program. Suggest ways to gather and implement client feedback to continuously improve the coaching experience."

Referral Program: "Develop a high-impact referral program that incentivizes my existing clients to refer new high-ticket clients. Include a tiered reward system, marketing materials for clients to share, and a follow-up sequence for referred leads. Provide ideas on how to seamlessly integrate this program into my client journey."

Remember, these prompts are your launchpad, not your limit. Feel free to tweak them, combine them, or use them as inspiration for your own. The key is to leverage AI to amplify your unique coaching superpowers.

Tips for Customization:

Niche-Specific Language: Incorporate terminology and concepts specific to your coaching niche. For example, a fitness coach might include terms like "macro tracking" or "progressive overload."

Client Pain Points: Weave your ideal client's specific challenges and desires into your prompts. The more detailed, the better!

Your Unique Methodology: If you have a signature process or framework, make sure to reference it in your prompts.

Brand Voice: Adjust the tone in your prompts to match your brand personality. Are you more formal and professional, or casual and friendly?

Troubleshooting Your Prompts:

Too Vague Results: If your AI responses are too general, try adding more specific details in your prompt. The more context, the better!

Off-Brand Tone: If the AI's tone doesn't match your brand voice, explicitly state the desired tone in your prompt. For example, "Use a conversational and empathetic tone."

Irrelevant Content: If the AI generates content that's not quite right for your audience, provide more details about your ideal client in the prompt.

Lack of Depth: For more comprehensive responses, ask the AI to "expand on" or "provide examples for" specific points.

Remember, creating effective prompts is a skill that improves with practice. Don't be afraid to iterate and refine your prompts based on the results you get. The more you use AI, the better you'll become at "speaking its language" and getting exactly what you need.

Now, go out there and start creating magic with these prompts. Your seven-figure coaching business is waiting for you to claim it. And hey, when you hit that seven-figure milestone (because I know you will), drop me a line. I can't wait to celebrate your success!

Key Takeaways:

- Implementing AI is a journey, not a destination - continuous learning and adaptation are key
- AI should enhance, not replace, your unique coaching skills and personal touch
- Start small with AI implementation and gradually expand as you gain confidence
- Measure the impact of AI on your business regularly and adjust your strategy accordingly
- Staying updated on AI advancements is crucial for maintaining a competitive edge
- Ethical considerations should always be at the forefront when using AI in coaching

Epilogue

The AI-Powered Future of Coaching

As we close the pages of this book, I want you to take a moment to imagine the future of your coaching business. Picture yourself confidently leveraging AI to create compelling content, engage with clients more meaningfully, and scale your impact beyond what you once thought possible.

This future isn't just a dream -- it's a reality that's unfolding right now. The AI revolution in coaching isn't coming; it's already here. And you, armed with the knowledge from this book, are at the forefront.

Remember when we started this journey? Perhaps you were skeptical about AI, or maybe you were excited but unsure where to begin. Now, you have a roadmap. You understand not just the "what" of AI in coaching, but the "how" and the "why."

But let me share a secret with you: The most powerful tool in your AI-enhanced coaching toolkit isn't any specific software or platform. It's your human touch -- your empathy, your intuition, your unique experiences and insights. AI is here to amplify these qualities, not replace them.

As you move forward, keep this in mind: AI is a powerful ally, but you are the true game-changer in your clients' lives. Use AI to handle the routine tasks, to gather insights, to create content -- but always infuse your work with your personal touch.

The coaching landscape will continue to evolve, and new AI tools will emerge. Stay curious. Keep learning. But most importantly, keep coaching. Because at the end of the day, it's not about the technology -- it's about the lives you're transforming.

You're not just building a coaching business; you're shaping the future of coaching itself. You're pioneering new ways to reach people, to understand them, to help them grow. And in doing so, you're growing too.

So, as you close this book and step into your AI-enhanced coaching future, remember this: The most important upgrade isn't happening in any software. It's happening in you. You're becoming a new kind of coach -- one who harnesses the power of AI to amplify your human gifts.

The future of coaching is bright, and you're lighting the way. I can't wait to see where this journey takes you.

Here's to your success, your growth, and the countless lives you'll transform with your AI-driven coaching. The future is yours to shape.

As you embark on this exciting journey, remember that you're not alone. Join our online community, attend AI-focused coaching workshops with us. The collective wisdom of your peers can be an invaluable resource as you navigate this new landscape.

And if you ever feel overwhelmed or unsure, remember why you started coaching in the first place. AI is here to enhance that purpose, not to change it. It's a tool to help you reach more people, make a bigger impact, and change more lives. Embrace it with curiosity and optimism, but never lose sight of the human element that makes coaching so powerful.

Looking ahead, I'm thrilled about the possibilities that emerging technologies might bring to our field. Imagine the potential of quantum computing in creating even more sophisticated coaching algorithms, or advanced neural networks that can provide deeper insights into client behavior. The future holds so much promise, and I'm committed to staying at the forefront of these developments to continue supporting coaches like you.

Reflecting on my own journey with AI, I'm amazed at how it has transformed not just my business, but my approach to coaching itself. It's made me a better listener, a more insightful guide, and has allowed me to impact more lives than I ever thought possible. I've seen clients achieve breakthroughs faster, implement changes more effectively, and reach their goals more consistently. And the best part? I have more time to focus on what I love most – connecting with my clients and helping them transform their lives and those they touch.

Now, it's your turn. Take that first step today. Whether it's signing up for an AI tool, revamping your content strategy, or reimagining your client experience, start small but dream big. Your AI-enhanced coaching journey begins now!

Remember, the goal isn't to become an AI expert overnight. It's to gradually integrate these powerful tools into your practice in a way that feels authentic and aligned with your coaching philosophy. Be patient with yourself, celebrate your successes (no matter how small), and learn from the challenges. Every step forward is progress.

As I fulfill my mission of helping people who help others, I encourage you to go forth and make a difference! Use the power of AI to amplify your impact, reach more clients, and create transformative experiences. The world needs your unique gifts now more than ever, and with AI as your ally, there's no limit to what you can achieve.

I can't wait to hear about your successes, your breakthroughs, and the lives you've changed with your AI-enhanced coaching. Remember, you're not just adapting to the future of coaching – you're creating it.

Here's to your amazing journey ahead!

Love, Lisa

Lisa Lieberman-Wang
The Coaches' Coach
AI Marketing & Business Expert

About The Author
Lisa Lieberman-Wang

AI Expert & Business Strategist
Speaker, Trainer, Seminar Leader
The Coaches' Coach

Lisa is a renowned Business & Marketing Strategist, known as "The Coaches' Coach." With over 40 years of experience advising and helping professionals succeed in their businesses, Lisa has mastered the art of increasing revenue, reducing operating expenses, and positioning her clients as leaders in their industries. Her unique ability to integrate personal growth with pragmatic business strategies has helped countless coaches and entrepreneurs achieve remarkable success.

Lisa is a certified expert in AI and Social Media, having completed advanced training programs that equip her with the latest tools and techniques in these fields. As an AI specialist, she leverages cutting-edge technology to create innovative solutions that transform businesses. Her expertise in social media ensures that her clients' brands are not only seen but also heard, creating a powerful online presence that drives engagement and growth.

Lisa's journey with AI began when she realized its potential to revolutionize the coaching industry. She immersed herself in the world of AI, experimenting with various tools and techniques in her own practice. Today, she uses AI to streamline her operations, create personalized coaching experiences, and generate data-driven insights that help her clients achieve breakthrough results.

In addition to her certifications in AI and social media, Lisa is a Licensed Master NLP (Neuro Linguist Programming) Practitioner & Trainer, author of several best-selling books, and a highly sought-after speaker. Trainer for Tony Robbins. She has an extensive background in sales, having personally achieved over $165 million in sales, personally and with her organization. Her commitment to continuous learning makes her a trailblazer in the coaching industry.

She has been featured in every major publication and on television stations such as ABC, CBS, NBC, FOX, The CW, Huffington Post, Harvard, and TEDx, and has been recognized as one of the "Top 25 Women Entrepreneurs" by Leading Women Entrepreneurs.

She helped create multiple six- and seven-figure revenues for entrepreneurs and brought tens of millions to the table for Fortune 500 companies. Lisa is also a multiple-time #1 best-selling author, the creator of FINE to FAB, Mastery to Millions Mastermind, and private Platinum Business Coaching.

Lisa's passion for helping others is evident in her dedication to her clients' success. She is not just a coach but a mentor, guiding her clients to achieve their ultimate business goals. With her innovative strategies and unwavering support, Lisa Lieberman-Wang is the go-to expert for anyone looking to elevate their coaching business and embrace the future of AI-powered success.

Looking ahead, Lisa envisions a future where AI and human expertise seamlessly blend to create unprecedented coaching experiences. She is committed to leading the charge in this AI revolution, ensuring that coaches around the world have the tools and knowledge they need to thrive in this exciting new era.

For more information about booking Lisa,
visit her website or call
1-877-250-7275 today.
Contact Info
www.LisaLiebermanWang.com
www.MasterytoMillions.com
www.FINEtoFAB.com

Email: Lisa@FINEtoFAB.com

Schedule a Call with Lisa at
www.CallwithLisa.com

Limited Offer

APPLY for a FREE Strategy Session

Lisa Lieberman-Wang invites you
or a friend to a private consultation.

To Apply go to
www.CallwithLisa.com
If you have no access to the internet,
Call 1-877-250-7275•

*The offer is open to all purchasers of How to Build a 7-Figure Coaching Business by Lisa Lieberman-Wang. The offer is limited to qualified individuals and availability of time in the schedule as deemed by Superlative Alternatives, Inc. Superlative Alternatives, Inc reserves the right to refuse strategy session to anyone it believes does not qualify. This is a limited time offer. The value of this FREE Strategy Session for you or a friend is $750 as of the time printed. Participants in the strategy session are under no additional financial obligation whatsoever to Superlative Alternatives, Inc. Free strategy session is not redeemable for cash.

Platinum Business Coaching

Your Fast Track to 7-Figure Success

Are you ready to elevate your coaching business to unprecedented heights? Look no further than the exclusive Platinum Business Coaching with Lisa Lieberman-Wang. With over 40 years of experience transforming businesses and a cutting-edge mastery of AI, Lisa knows what it takes to skyrocket your revenue, optimize your operations, and position you as the undisputed leader in your niche.

What sets this program apart?

1. **AI-Powered Strategies:** Leverage Lisa's expertise in AI to create a competitive edge that puts you light years ahead of your competition.
2. **Personalized Success Blueprint:** Get a custom-tailored roadmap designed specifically for your business, your goals, and your unique strengths.
3. **High-Impact Marketing Mastery:** Learn how to attract high-ticket clients effortlessly using Lisa's proven "7-Figure Talk That Sells" methodology.
4. **Scaling Secrets Unveiled:** Discover how to grow your business exponentially without burning out or sacrificing your personal life.
5. **VIP Access:** Enjoy direct access to Lisa's vast network of industry secrets, and game-changing resources.

Here's what you'll master:

- **Differentiating Your Brand:** Stand out in a crowded market with a unique positioning that magnetizes your ideal clients.
- **Maximizing Your Intellectual Property:** Create and leverage your IP to build multiple revenue streams.
- **Perfect Client Precision:** Identify and effortlessly attract your dream clients who value your expertise and gladly pay premium prices.
- **High-Converting Sales Funnels:** Design irresistible offers and automated systems that sell while you sleep.
- **AI-Enhanced Client Experience:** Deliver personalized, high-touch service at scale using cutting-edge AI tools.

Exclusive Bonuses:

- **2-Hour VIP Discovery Session:** Spend a focused time with Lisa to create a custom plan for your business goals.
- **Weekly Private Coaching:** Regular check-ins with Lisa to review progress and make necessary adjustments.
- **Network Access:** Tap into Lisa's extensive team of resources to help grow your business.
- **AI Tool Suite:** Curated by Lisa
- **Customized Tools:** Use templates and tools tailored to streamline your processes and increase efficiency.
- Lifetime Access to Program Updates
- **Monthly Virtual Assistance:** Implement your needs with included virtual assistant support. (Allotted hours given monthly.)

This high-touch, results-driven program is not for everyone. Lisa only works with a select group of committed coaches ready to play big and create a massive impact.

Are you ready to join the elite circle of 7-figure coaches?

Spots are extremely limited. Apply now for a complimentary strategy session to see if you're a fit for this transformative program.

Warning: This program is known to create exponential business growth. Only apply if you're ready for massive success!

Apply Now for Your Complimentary Strategy Session at
www.CallwithLisa.com

Don't wait. Your 7-figure coaching empire awaits!

If you're ready to take your business to the next level and achieve your ultimate goals, the Platinum Business Coaching program is your perfect choice. Apply now for your strategy session and start your journey to success today.

Apply Now for a Complimentary Strategy Session at
www.CallwithLisa.com

Contact Info:
www.LisaLiebermanWang.com

Praise for Mastery to Millions™ & Platinum Business Coaching

"Lisa has been a game-changer for our business. As a platinum business coaching client, I have witnessed her unparalleled expertise in transforming abstract ideas into thriving ventures with remarkable results. Her strategic insights and innovative use of AI have been instrumental in our success.

With Lisa's expert guidance, we built a robust relationship coaching practice for my wife and me. She meticulously helped us develop our website, landing page, content, blogs, eBooks, social media presence, and scripts, all leveraging cutting-edge AI tools. The transformation was extraordinary, and our online presence became significantly more impactful and engaging.

Lisa's expertise didn't stop there. She also crafted an extraordinary marketing strategy for our Airbnb in Puerto Rico, utilizing AI to maximize our reach and retention. Her ability to generate captivating material and content that attracts and retain clients is truly exceptional. Even identified influencers we have partnered with to expand our reach.

Following Lisa's proven plans, we delivered a 7-Figure Talk That Sells, each generating five figures. Her deep knowledge, innovative approach, and unwavering dedication have profoundly impacted our business success. Thanks to Lisa, we've seen a dramatic increase in our client base and revenue. I can't recommend her enough for anyone looking to grow their business and achieve extraordinary results."

– Frankie,
Relationship Coach and Hacienda Serena,
PR Airbnb Owner

"When I first started coaching with Lisa Lieberman-Wang, I realized within the 1st month that it was the BEST investment I have made in myself in the last 12 years.

Since working with her, I made over $420,000 in the first year working with Lisa. To be honest, I am not shocked. Lisa knows how to look at what you are doing and how to make it better. She knows how to leverage resources that you may have never thought of.

If you are looking to take your business to another level, learn new ways to leverage, and how to create more income, Lisa is a MUST."

– Veenu Keller,
Parent/Child Peacemaker

"About 2 years ago I took the Tony Robbins online program KBB, The Knowledge Business Blueprint and I finished but I got stuck because I guess you're supposed to figure it out after that on your own.

I'm so fortunate I met Lisa... I took her online business program master to millions and her platinum coaching and the very first week after I was done with the program, I made $23,000." Followed by a high six figures in the following months. "Lisa, I'm blessed by you and can't wait to be making more money with you."

– Magie Cook,
Food Business Strategist,
Keynote Speaker, Nobel Prize Winner

"I have been starting and stopping for the last few years, and Lisa got me off the block. She got me moving forward and selling my program. So, I'm extremely grateful for everything you've done for me, the business, and the overall vision of where I see myself in five years.

"One of the biggest takeaways was the way we broke down topics like sales and psychology. I had thought I understood the formatting for how to present information. But then to make small tweaks to then also have it be persuasive enough that people are like, "Hey, I want to learn more." They're leaning into you instead of you chasing them around. That was incredible.

"And then, after understanding how the entire process works, Lisa literally brought me behind the scenes and gave me exclusive access to everything you do. And by seeing that, it gave me more context so that when I was actually moving forward, I knew the next steps that I was going to be moving into and could actually get results.

"She is methodical and knows how to help you create talks that sell. Her training is worth millions.

"Anyone who wants to get the message out there, who has something valuable for people and can help them, Lisa is the person to go to because she knows how to get that message out for you and how to keep you engaged, passionate, and pushing forward about your dreams and goals to achieve them.

"Invest in yourself. Put yourself around people who know what to do and can get you to the next level, and that's Lisa Lieberman-Wang. Make the investment so that you can stop talking about it and start doing it!"

– Oliver Fernandez,
Wealth with Multifamily Real Estate

"I love Lisa. Lisa has the most authentic, loving, and amazing way of interacting with me. I went from having a fear of building my own business to really feeling like I could do it. And I have that hand-holding level of support that I need to get all of my questions answered. She has a step-by-step process that I can follow and know that there is a system in place to really help me with my business, and in several months of working with Lisa, I made over $20,000. And it has been a most amazing experience. I would 100% recommend that if you are growing a business or working through fears and obstacles, Lisa is that person for you."

– Katie Sisk,
Epilepsy Specialist

"I've been working with Lisa Lieberman-Wang for the last year, in her platinum program. I have a business program called "I Am Ready" that has been in the works for four years. And, what took me four years to develop, she's been able to help me launch and promote in six months.

"It's been phenomenal for me. I was also very impressed with the fact that I had done a program I thought was a couple of million-dollar business, but now that I got it up and running, it is north of 25 million. It is fully functioning, so I really appreciate everything. I'm continuing forward, and I can't say enough. 'Thank you, Lisa.'"

– Larissa Krishok,
Founder & CEO, I AM Ready

"I want to share my personal experience with Lisa Lieberman-Wang and the Mastery to Millions program. It was such a powerful experience.

"Within the first two days, I took her framework from her signature talk and followed the formula exactly. I sent it to one client who instantly signed.

"So, within an instant, in my opinion, her services were so valuable. So, if you're even thinking about it or questioning it, trust your gut and hire Lisa Lieberman-Wang. You won't regret it. Thanks."

– Kerry Preston,
Founder & CEO Growtality

"My greatest success working with Lisa was getting my first client just as we were starting. That was really good because it showed me the effectiveness of the program. I love everything about it; it's beautiful, and particularly I love having a very effective structure for getting my program online. Launching my business—that's what I love about this executive coaching because I'm getting a lot of clarity about the path that I need to take. With my first client, I got $10,000 for just seven hours of speaking. I'm very excited about that because we are just starting and I already sold my first program to a company, and it's very well paid as well, which is very good. That's my first success and I am sure more is coming."

– Elizabeth Cruz,
Wealth & Finance Specialist

"I love working with Lisa because I was stuck with what I knew I wanted to do with my business. And I've had a business for several years, but I've just been doing an hourly thing and stressing out over it. I needed someone to give me that push and to hold my hand.

"I did my first webinar, I sold three of my Cut the Crap Packages that I haven't even put together yet. I have people now that are signing up. I've made over five figures and I haven't really done too much work but talked to somebody on the phone a few times and now know what to say and how to say it. The systems she teaches are priceless and help me leverage my time and energy in my business."

— Amie Osborn,
Fitness & Nutrition Specialist

"I just wanted to thank you so much for helping me out. It's truly been a pleasure; you've been an incredible coach... You've taught me a lot, and I really appreciate it.

"Our OTC (over the counter) sales have increased drastically by 50 to 100% increase. And we also did really well with marketing. I was very hesitant to market because I'm always nervous that I'm pushing information on people. And you helped me reframe that so that I'm educating. And that I have a service that I'm providing...

"I was very scared to do the signature talk. That was a huge win for me to get in front of people and just say what I knew. I wouldn't have done it without you, that's for sure. We had a 5-figure launch with our new weight loss product.

"We were just thinking about that the other day, "Wow, we always wanted to have a high-ticket item that we could provide a lot of value to our patients with, and we couldn't figure out what it could possibly be so to be able to give them something that's helping them out so much where they're getting off medications. They are feeling better, and they have more energy. They don't need to go to the doctor as much. They're not as scared for COVID to be able to offer all that, and to have turned that into a revenue stream has been amazing. It's been really cool."

— Rebecca Holt,
Pharmacy Owner & Founder of Weight Loss Product

Your testimonial is waiting for you here.
We look forward to helping you build your own
7 figure-coaching business too!

Love, Lisa

www.LisaLiebermanWang.com

www.MasterytoMillions.com

Bonus Book
www.HowtoBuilda7FigureCoachingBusiness.com

Follow Me On Social Media
Facebook, LinkedIn, Instagram, TikTok, YouTube

@LLiebermanWang

www.ingramcontent.com/pod-product-compliance
Lightning Source LLC
LaVergne TN
LVHW051244050326
832903LV00028B/2568